MW01257978

FINITE INTUITION

MILO DE ANGELIS

Finite Intuition:
Selected Poetry and Prose

Edited and Translated by
Lawrence Venuti

LOS ANGELES
SUN & MOON PRESS
1995

Sun & Moon Press
A Program of The Contemporary Arts Educational Project, Inc.
a nonprofit corporation
6026 Wilshire Boulevard, Los Angeles, California 90036

This edition first published in paperback in 1995 by Sun & Moon Press
10 9 8 7 6 5 4 3 2 1
FIRST EDITION
©1995 by Milo De Angelis
Translation and Introduction ©1995 by Lawrence Venuti
The Italian texts first appeared in the following books:
Somiglianze (Milano: Ugo Guanda Editore, 1976) ©1976 by Milo De Angelis
Poesia e destino (Bologna: Cappelli Editore, 1982) ©1982 by Milo De Angelis
Millimetri (Torino: Giulio Einuadi Editore, 1983) ©1983 by Milo De Angelis
Terra del viso (Milano: Arnoldo Mondadori Editore, 1985) ©1985 by Milo De Angelis
Distante un padre (Milano: Arnoldo Mondadori Editore, 1989) ©1989 by Milo De Angelis
Reprinted with permission of the above publishers and the author.
Biographical material ©1995 by Sun & Moon Press
All rights reserved

Grateful acknowledgement is made to the following publications where these translations first
appeared, some in substantially different versions: *Alea, American Poetry Review, Chicago
Review, Object, Painted Bride Quarterly, Paris Review, Partisan Review, Poetry, Poetry East,
Seneca Review, Stand, Sulfur, Texture, Washington Review, Italian Poetry Today*, edited by Ruth
Feldman and Brian Swann (St. Paul, Minnesota: New Rivers Press, 1979), and *New Italian
Poets*, edited by Dana Gioia and Michael Palma (Brownsville, Oregon: Story Line Press, 1991).
Portions of the introduction appeared in somewhat different form in *Dictionary of Literary
Biography: Twentieth-Century Italian Poets, SubStance*, and *Washington Review*.

This book was made possible, in part, through an operational grant from the
Andrew W. Mellon Foundation, through a production grant and through contributions to
The Contemporary Arts Educational Project, Inc.,
a nonprofit corporation

Cover: unknown artist, The Maryland
Institute College of Art
Cover Design: Katie Messborn
Typography: Guy Bennett

LIBRARY OF CONGRESS CATALOGING IN PUBLICATION DATA
De Angelis, Milo (1951)
[Selections. English. 1995]
Finite Intitution: Selected Poetry and Prose / Milo De Angelis;
edited and translated by Lawrence Venuti.—1st ed.
p. cm — (Sun & Moon Classics: 65)
Translation of selected poems and essays originally published
in Italian between 1976 and 1989.
ISBN: 1-55713-068-X : $11.95
1. De Angelis, Milo, 1951 —Translations into English.
1. Venuti, Lawrence. 11. Title. 111. Series.
PQ4864.E19A28 1995
811'.54—dc20
94-44513
CIP

Printed in the United States of America on acid-free paper.

For Lindsay

forderst du alles
in seine Aura

Contents

II MILLIMETERS

III LAND OF THE FACE

Introduction

> *Just as every man's wife cannot escape*
> *a theory of translating, so every trans-*
> *lation shows, with no possibility of es-*
> *cape, in its interlinear spasm, whether*
> *its marriage with a poet is truly nec-*
> *essary.*
>
> —MILO DE ANGELIS

The problematic status of every translation arises from
the fact that the translator must labor over an inescap-
able cultural difference. Translating means negotiating
between two disparate languages, but this act of negotia-
tion cannot proceed without confronting the disparity
between two cultural contexts and the conflicting respon-
sibilities they impose on the translator. On the one hand,
the translator assumes the responsibility to produce a text
that is intelligible to the target-language reader. Readabil-
ity is in fact the motive and guiding principle for bringing
foreign writing into another language, and it endows the
translation with an element of familiarity, engaging the
reader in a process of identification which constitutes un-
derstanding. The reader understands the translation not
simply because it is written in a language he or she knows
and recognizes, but because the language is in varying de-
grees allusive, laden with familiar connotations, woven
with connections to familiar cultural products and prac-

tices. Because the principle of readability answers to the
reader's needs, it results in a translation that is intelligible
but imperfect, never an equivalent with an exact fit to the
foreign writing, always a ragged-edged reproduction that
both loses some source-language meanings and adds oth-
ers specific to the target-language culture.

On the other hand, however, the translator has the
responsibility to produce a text that respects the integrity
of the foreign writing. This includes reproducing its for-
mal and semantic qualities as closely as possible, but also
preserving its alien nature by developing techniques of
estrangement which foreground linguistic and cultural
differences. To meet this responsibility to the source-lan-
guage text, the translator must stop the target-language
culture from so domesticating it as to be guilty of a cul-
tural narcissism that betrays imperialistic tendencies. It is
this domestication that always threatens by adhering to
the principle of readability: since readable translation re-
quires the translator to pursue an identity, a self-recogni-
tion, it risks discovering only the same culture in foreign
writing, only the same self in the cultural other. And yet
since respect for the integrity of foreign writing requires
the translator to pursue difference, it too carries a risk—
namely incomprehension. Hence, the translator's work is
deeply, some would say impossibly, conflicted: he or she
must write a text that is sufficiently recognizable to the
target-language reader to be understood, but that at the
same time is sufficiently estranging to suggest something
of the irreducible foreignness of the source-language text
and its culture.

Translating the poetry and prose of the Italian writer
Milo De Angelis poses in a most acute way the problems
inherent in this dual task. The European cultural tradi-

tion in which his writing emerged differs radically from the tradition that has dominated Anglo-American poetry for centuries, although with notable deviations. And this difference creates recalcitrant difficulties for his English-language translator, demanding a translation strategy that, in its effort to reproduce the Italian texts, simultaneously falls short of and exceeds those texts in ways that can frustrate the Anglo-American reader searching for the recognizable. For these reasons, it seems that the most useful introduction to De Angelis's poems and essays is first to consider the European cultural tradition that informs and is transformed by them and then to explain the strategy I have used in my translations.

*

Born in 1951 in Milan, Milo De Angelis is a sophisticated experimentalist who has set out to reinvent poetry in postmodern terms. His work since the beginning of the 1970s is a series of stunning poetic researches that draw on classical literature, existential phenomenology, and psychoanalysis, but rethink them according to the new conceptions of subjectivity and language that underlie the variety of poststructuralisms in contemporary French and Italian culture.

In De Angelis's writing, Martin Heidegger's attempt to overcome the western metaphysical tradition and discover an originary thinking about human existence is joined to several arguments associated with Friedrich Nietzsche and Jacques Lacan, particularly the critique of morality and representation as potent inventions of "value" and "truth" and the exposure of subjectivity as a linguistic construction in which desire is repressed by the very means of its expression. This configuration of ideas establishes the fundamental paradox of De Angelis's poetic project. He strives to free the anarchic origins of existence from the cultural and social determinations that order and normalize it through language. At the same time, however, he is constantly aware that the origins remain ineffable, outside of the poem, because it is language that imposes order and normalcy, negating what it names, restraining what exceeds it, bringing the illusory comforts of intelligibility, coherence, and transparency to calm the panic of the unknown. For De Angelis, the function of poetry is to stimulate originary thinking by pushing at the limits of language and transgressing cultural norms, but always with the awareness that their destruction is simultaneously tragic and creative, the end of existence and the ceaseless proliferation of new beginnings. His poems stage what the poet and critic Giuseppe Conte described as a common project for Italian poetry in the 1970s: a "liberation which is unchaining and silence, irresponsibility and joy, attainment, through loss, of the infinite simplicity of things."[1] Over the past twenty years, De Angelis has been exploring these ideas in a powerful body of writing, strangely disquieting in its stylistic dislocations and its reflections on human consciousness and action, profound in its evocation of a peculiarly postmodern sense of tragedy.

De Angelis develops the formal experimentation characteristic of the so-called neoavantgarde literary movements which surfaced in Italy during the late 1950s and early 1960s and can be charted in magazines like Luciano Anceschi's *Il Verri*, founded in 1956, and in polemical anthologies like Alfredo Giuliani's *I Novissimi: poesie per gli anni '60 (The Newest: Poetry for the Sixties,*

1961). Giuliani's preface outlines the *Novissimi*'s project
as a materialist cultural politics: language is fractured in
a "'schizomorphic' vision" which simultaneously reflects
and resists the mental dislocations and illusory representa-
tions of consumer capitalism.[2] Giuliani asserts that for
him, as for the other poets in his anthology (Elio Pagliarini,
Edoardo Sanguineti, Nanni Balestrini, and Antonio Porta),
poetry is a subversion of the dominant ideology, what he
calls "the unmasking, challenging the silence that always
follows, along with the idle talk, the deterioration of lan-
guage, exasperating the nonsense, refusing the oppression
of imposed meanings, relating with taste and with love
the thoughts and lies of this schizophrenic age" (p. xvi).
De Angelis shares the *Novissimi*'s view that discontinu-
ous form is the most suitable way to address philosophi-
cal problems raised by language, representation, and
subjectivity. But he eschews the explicit political engage-
ment with which the neoavantgarde treated these prob-
lems for a poetic discourse that is both deeply personal
and densely philosophical. De Angelis's more speculative
treatment is suggestive of Heidegger's thinking. As the
poet and critic Franco Fortini noticed, the poems in De
Angelis's first collection, *Somiglianze* (*Resemblances*,
1976), show him "fascinated with the Heideggerian vorti-
ces of origin, absence, recurrence, and the danger of
death."[3]

   De Angelis's divergence from the neoavantgarde can
be suggested in a brief comparison with Sanguineti. In
Purgatorio de l'Inferno (*The Purgatory of Hell*, 1964),[4] for
example, Sanguineti questions the idea that language can
be a transparent representation of reality by exposing its
complicating social determinations, here the economic
interests that mediate such books as might be read to a

child, but that the adult reader must make visible through
a provocatively discontinuous catalogue of images:

> this is Puss-in-Boots, this is the Peace of Barcelona
> between Charles V and Clement VII, a locomotive, a
> blossoming peach tree, a sea-horse: but if you turn
> the page, Alessandro, you can see the money:
> [...]

Sanguineti's poem is informed by a Brechtian strategy
of defamiliarizing everyday cultural products and prac-
tices to expose the social contradictions in which they are
implicated. Typical of the *Novissimi* poets, Sanguineti
relies so much on common contemporary language that
his text becomes in effect a "found" object, perhaps a
parent's bed-time story to a child, although with the aim
of opening up this domestic discourse to a range of social
determinations. His *Purgatorio de l'Inferno*, like much of
his poetry, is a frenetic *tranche de vie*, a rapidly passing
stream of diaristic passages, episodes in the poet's personal
life, excerpts and applications of his readings in philoso-
phy, literature, psychology, and political theory, punctu-
ated by left-wing commentary on social issues. Giuliani's
prefatory remarks describe Sanguineti's style as "con-
stantly converting historical and psychological terms into
one another" (p. xx).

The critique of representation in De Angelis's poetry is
not articulated in historical materialist terms, but rather
based on Heidegger's concept of "being-towards-death,"
which De Angelis submits to a Nietzschean revision. In
Being and Time (1927), Heidegger argues that human ex-
istence is perpetually "falling," always already determined

by concernful relations with people and things, its identity dispersed into the "they"—until the possibility of death appears.[5] The anticipation of death, the possibility of being nothing, constitutes a "limit-situation," in which the subject is forced to recognize the inauthenticity of its determinate nature and gains "a freedom which has been released from the Illusions of the 'they,' and which is factical, certain of itself, and anxious" (p. 311).

In the programmatic poem "The Central Idea," De Angelis exploits the potential for drama in this climactic moment of truth by sketching a hospital scene. The poem depicts being-towards-death as a state of physical and psychological extremity where the apparent unity of lived experience is split by competing representations, and consciousness loses its self-possession and self-consistency. "Actions" are decentered from intentionality: "their meaning" is never uniquely appropriate to the subject, but an appropriation by the "they," figured here as the "bosses" who are so "threatening" to identity because they speak "in a dream," having even colonized the unconscious. The "central idea" seems to be that subjectivity is ultimately "nothing," mere action on which meaning is imposed, an ensemble of biological processes whose meaninglessness "despotic beings" inadvertently reveal when they attempt to impose meaning through scientific representations like x-rays. The formal peculiarities of this text—the shifts from realistic detail to abstract reflection to quoted statement, the scanty amount of information, the fragmented syntax—mimic the identity-shattering experience of being-towards-death by destabilizing the signifying process, abandoning any linearity of meaning and unbalancing the reader's search for intelligibility. What does become clear, however, is that De Angelis's poem resists any suggestion

that being-towards-death is the prelude to authentic ex-
istence as Heidegger conceives it, being that is unified and
free, that is "something of its own" and can "'choose' it-
self and win itself" (*Being and Time*, p. 68). In form and
theme, "The Central Idea" rather reflects Nietzsche's cor-
rosive notes in *The Will to Power*, where human agency is
described as "no subject but an action, a positing, creative,
no 'causes and effects.'"[6]

The limit-situations in De Angelis's poetry are experi-
ences that challenge consciousness, that threaten or sus-
pend its rational coherence, that break down its self-iden-
tity and give it access to what is other than itself. The
situations that recur most often include not only the brush
with death, whether through accident, illness, or a suicide
attempt, but also psychological suffering, sexual desire,
drug intoxication, biological process, the intellectual im-
maturity of childhood, and the unreflective spontaneity
of athletic performance. These are situations of transgres-
sion because they are pre-linguistic or they fracture or
abandon language, releasing subjectivity from its web of
determinations, allowing it to deviate from the concepts
of rationality and moral value that shape it, revealing not
only the unwillingness of these concepts to permit devia-
tion or admit difference, but also their fragile basis in the
interaction between language and consciousness. Hence,
subjectivity in De Angelis's poetry is volatile and in pro-
cess, often presented in dramatic scenes with snippets of
dialogue and a rapid succession of evocative images. Me-
tonymy is the dominant mode of representing this experi-
ence, and the rush of metonymic representations can be
movingly resonant, even as their speed and heterogeneity
endanger communication. The discontinuous form of De
Angelis's poetry serves to evoke a notion of consciousness

not as the stable, coherent origin of meaning, knowledge, and action, but as constituted by its contradictory conditions, by language, by familial relationships, by the culture at large, but needing the limit-situation to be reminded of these forgotten conditions and to imagine the new possibilities in them.

The voice (or voices?) in "The Train Corridor" is apparently engaged in a strange lover's quarrel, both bitter and very abstract, where desire is structured by conflicting strategies of representation, but ultimately breaks them down. Although never clearly defined as a distinct identity, the quarrelsome voice at the opening opposes a concept of "love" governed by "resemblance" or sameness in the lovers, and seems to favor an alternate one governed by difference, or deviation, the invention of new "expectations." Yet the next quotation, "you're still there," can signify the introduction of another voice, suggesting that maybe the one who hurled the accusation of "plagiary" should be changing its expectations, maybe the accuser should be abandoning any search for the authentic existence, any effort to avoid the dishonesty of imitation. The insistent, anonymous questioning proceeds to the Nietzschean argument that love is yet another form of the will to power, where two lovers are locked in a struggle for domination and can "confute" each other, can impose a representation that "will be true" for both. At this point, the voices lose what vague definition they may have acquired as the text unfolded, and the two conflicting positions of intelligibility are finally abandoned by the last voice, full of expectation for another, still unspoken "word" that will construct a new subject-position for "the body," a new relationship for the biological "force" that sustains yet threatens the linguistic basis of every such relationship. The poem treats desire as at once driving language use and depending on language for its articulation, but also, following Lacan, as undergoing a repression in the process, an exclusion of other loves, other expectations, other worlds.[7]

The concept of subjectivity as a determinate process makes De Angelis's poetry deeply sceptical of established moral values, leading him to adopt a morality based on Nietzsche's concept of tragedy. If the "world," as Nietzsche argues in *The Will to Power*, "is 'in flux,' as something in a state of becoming, as a falsehood always changing but never getting near the truth," then an "active" morality is required, a willingness to accept deviation, a joyful affirmation of multiplicity and uncertainty, an experimental creation of new values, "as a counterweight to this extreme fatalism" (pp. 330, 546). But insofar as this creativity depends on the transgression of limits, the deviation from cultural norms, the annihilation of individuality, its joy exists simultaneously with suffering. In *The Birth of Tragedy*, Nietzsche discovers this suffering in Greek tragedy and describes it as "Dionysian," as "a clash of different worlds, e.g. of a divine and human one," in which the hero "suffers in his own person the primordial contradiction that is concealed in things."[8] The impact of these ideas on De Angelis's thinking can be seen in the essay "Twentieth-Century Tragedy" from his theoretical and critical work, *Poesia e destino* (*Poetry and Fate*, 1982). Here, in a phrase borrowed from Hegel, tragedy is defined as "the collision between telos and contingency." Yet De Angelis's formulation is less Hegelian than Nietzschean in its treatment of this collision as one that rules out transcendence, that exposes the limitations of human subjectivity, but welcomes them as conditions of new possibility, refusing to resolve them in an idealist metaphysics. What is tragic about the subject is that it cannot transcend its contradictory determinations to gain immediate access to an essential truth, cannot return to some original unity. For De Angelis, tragedy is "what continues to end." The project of his poetry, then, is to proliferate and intensify the contradictions by abnegating the self, affirming difference, inventing, willing, cultivating what Nietzsche in *The Birth of Tragedy* calls the "Dionysian art" through which the voice of "nature" can be heard: "Be as I am! Amid the ceaseless flux of phenomena I am the eternally creative primordial mother, eternally impelling to existence, eternally finding satisfaction in this change of phenomena!" (p. 104).

Several of De Angelis's poems indicate the fundamentally affirmative significance of this concept of tragedy by consecrating transgression and linking it to the natural cycle of birth, death, and rebirth. In "The Assassins," violence, a limit-situation in which human action drifts from social identity toward the realm of becoming, is said to have a "season," but also a "sacred wait" and a moment of "solemnity," whereby the temporality of nature is transformed into a religious ceremony. In "Neither Point Nor Line," the "sacred wait" is a Buddhist abandonment of rationality for physical process:

> light zen, in the field,
> the force that held the birds in flight
> (an interruption and they would fall)
> becomes the hell of counting them.

"The Dream of the Dancing Cat" expresses a similar piety toward the recurrence of nature, but in this case the

imagery is suggestive of the Eleusinian Mysteries, the cult
of the fertile goddess Demeter. The "lady of sea and grain"
speaks in a way that is god-like, that challenges the deter-
minations of human existence, whether biological ("as if
she had never existed") or social ("without need of guaran-
tees"). This limit-situation occurs "in the plain/of light,"
an allusion to the divine effulgence that, according to
Plutarch, lit the hierophant at the most secret Eleusinian
rite.9 Yet there is also the sinister suggestion of criminal-
ity in the "swift shadow" of the woman, travelling under
cover of the night, her voice a "threatening hiss." The title
of the poem refers to the Hollywood western, *The Man
Who Loved Cat Dancing* (1973), in which a woman leaves
her husband to ride with a band of outlaws. The lady of
sea and grain personifies De Angelis's tragic concept of
nature as contradiction, transgression, violation, and the
rich allusiveness of the text, its mixing of elite and mass
culture, serves as a reminder that it offers no more than a
simulacrum of nature, a mediated representation which
exposes and simultaneously contradicts its cultural con-
ditions because it can never transcend them. The imagery
that connects nature, violence, and female recurs in "the
woman warrior" of "Stones in the Warm Mud" from *Re-
semblances* and in the "matron-at-arms" of "Born on the
earth," a poem from De Angelis's second collection,
Millimetri (*Millimeters*, 1983).

Millimeters shows a marked increase in the rapid
discontinuity of De Angelis's poetry as he explores the
murky origins and vicissitudes of subjectivity against the
natural cycle. The penchant for staging dramatic scenes
gives way to highly elliptical patterns of imagery, as in
"Now she is unadorned," where the images are complex,
yet consistent with the philosophical speculation of De

Angelis's first book. References to agriculture, suicide, and religious ritual are combined with surreal juxtapositions ("handfuls" of "years," "a field" with "a hollow head") to suggest the key idea that nature is creative only insofar as it is violent and self-destructive. The rapidity and resonance of the images and the sudden shifts in the syntax give this and other poems from *Millimeters* an obscure but exhilarating power, eliciting the sort of experience that Nietzsche finds in Dionysian art: "we are really for a brief moment primordial being itself, feeling its raging desire for existence and joy in existence; the struggle, the pain, the destruction of phenomena, now appear necessary to us, in view of the excess of countless forms of existence which force and push one another into life, in view of the exuberant fertility of the universal will" (*The Birth of Tragedy*, p. 104). The paradox, however, is that to be primordially is to be nothing, dissolved in the ceaseless flux of becoming; being depends on discourse, on naming: it is "baptism" that gives "a breath" to "the myriads."

De Angelis's combination of discontinuous form with originary thinking displays his strong affinity with Paul Celan's poetry. In Celan's speech "The Meridian" (1960), the obscurity of his and other contemporary poetry—what he calls "the difficulties of vocabulary, the faster flow of syntax or a more awakened sense of ellipsis"—is associated with a reconsideration of the lyric poem.[10] Celan locates a contradiction in the lyric project of personal expression, of evoking an individual voice: the poem "speaks only on its own, its very behalf," he states, but it "has always hoped, for this very reason, to speak also on behalf of the *strange* [...] on behalf of the other, who knows, perhaps of an *altogether other*" (p. 48). The poem alienates the individual self by liberating it from its familiar boundaries, becoming "the place where the person was able to set himself free as an—estranged—I," but where "along with the I, estranged and freed *here, in this manner,* some other thing is also set free"—free from the appropriating power of the speaking "I," of a personal language (pp. 46, 47). The poem does not transcend but acknowledges the contradiction between self-expression and communication with some other: it is "language actualized, set free under the sign of a radical individuation which, however, remains as aware of the limits drawn by language as of the possibilities it opens" (p. 49).

De Angelis follows Celan's transformation of the lyric by developing a poetics of the limit-situation, but one which derives from a modern movement in Italian poetry, the hermeticism that dominated the 1930s and 1940s. In the essay "Starting a New Line: An Autobiographical Note," De Angelis describes his early interest in the formal innovations of hermeticism, its oblique means of signification, particularly the ambiguities released by the "subtle attention to pauses and juxtapositions" in the poems of Mario Luzi, Alfonso Gatto, and Piero Bigongiari. De Angelis's strategy, however, is to exaggerate the hermetic fragmentation of meaning, so that the very form of his poems can enact the originary thinking that is their theme, the tragic collision between telos and contingency. The telos of poetic composition, "what preexists" and radically determines its meaning, includes not only the rules of syntax, the "sentence," but also the experience chosen for representation and the elaborate signifying structures or "poetics" typical of literary texts. De Angelis introduces the contingent with syntactical irregularities, abrupt caesurae and enjambments, shifts in discourse, all of which are circumscribed by, but nonetheless alien to, the telos already animating the composition. The effect of these apparently aleatory procedures is to break down the process of signification in the text, making it a site of incipient meanings and structures, turning it into the verbal equivalent of "the plain/of light" mentioned in "The Dream of the Dancing Cat," fertile with new interpretive possibilities that invite the reader to participate in the creative flux of textuality. Although De Angelis's use of sound imagery gives his account of poetic composition an oracular quality, he avoids the transcendence implied in the Heideggerian "call" of authentic existence, the primordial unity of being. De Angelis's "dictation" is rather a mythologization of a material textual practice: it results in the polysemy that admits difference to the text and brings it to its own limits, the voice that is not the poet's and therefore threatens his individuality even as it traces the contours of a poetics, an experience, a subject. Hence, De Angelis's poetry often takes as a point of departure specific episodes in his own life, but his originary poetics renders them impersonal, thickening the representation with an intricate network of images and allusions, resisting any facile reduction of the text to authorial biography.

De Angelis's third collection of poetry, *Terra del viso* (*Land of the Face*, 1985), is a rich synthesis of these poetic researches. Some poems show a return to the suspenseful dramatic style of *Resemblances*; others show the impact of the heterogeneous and fragmentary images that characterize *Millimeters*. The speculations on subjectivity examine a wider range of human experiences and relationships, including infancy and childhood, and the autobiographical references are at times more explicit, as in "Conversation with Father" and "Talking to Dario." The result is a provocative meditation on human temporality in remarkably inventive verse. "Foreweb" posits "a styleless time" to represent subjectivity as a fragile cultural construct, vulnerable to physiological changes. "Will You Put on the Blindfold?" is a dramatic monologue that sketches a limit-situation in childhood: two boys are jumping across the roofs of houses. It is the poet's persona who is the more Dionysian of the two, who urges the other to jump blindfolded, to act without reflection, to become mere biological process like the "creepers" and carry the "corncob," symbolic of the goddess of fertility. The poem avoids the romantic idealization of childhood as happy and innocent, privileged by its proximity to nature and its distance from adult concerns; instead, the youthful persona is depicted as knowingly reckless, aware that to be like the "creeping brothers" he must fearlessly risk death in a ritualistic game made all the more alarming by his excited, childlike tone.

The question of temporality enters De Angelis's poems not only through recurrent images drawn from biology, but also formally, through the very recurrence of the imagery. To understand the momentary limit-situations and the instants of dense polysemy, the reader is led to construct intertextual relationships, initially among De Angelis's texts, but also between them and the other cultural materials they appropriate. As a consequence, reading his poems forces an awareness of how language and subjectivity are constituted in time, by their difference within a cultural tradition.

De Angelis's use of the color blue, for example, transforms image patterns in Celan's poems which themselves respond to earlier, romantic and modern uses of this color to signify the imagination or the absolute (e.g. Novalis's *die blaue Blume*, Mallarmé's *azure*). Celan's "Isleward" (1955) performs a postmodern critique of these transcen-

dental meanings by associating blue with winter and
death, foreignness and isolation, calling attention to the
boundaries that both enable and limit identity:

> so the foreign, the free ones row,
> the masters of ice and of stone:
> chimed at by sinking buoys,
> barked at by shark-blue ocean.[11]

Celan's blue works by metaphorizing a naturalistic de-
tail, offering the reader a foothold for interpretation. In
several of De Angelis's poems, however, the color recurs
at points of opacity which depend for meaning on earlier
texts like Celan's, but deepen his thinking about the deter-
minations of subjectivity. Thus, the "breeze/ blue and dar-
kling" in "Foreweb" is connected to the "styleless time,"
where consciousness has not yet received definition, or
where it slips through the constraints of law (the uncer-
tainty over whether "a crime" was "committed or wit-
nessed") and gender (the injury which "stitches male back
to female"). The intertextuality of De Angelis's poems situ-
ates them and the reader in a cultural tradition and thereby
projects a concept of temporality quite like the "recursive-
ness" which Susan Stewart discovers in John Ashbery's
poetry, "where language examines its own conditions of
emergence and disappearance within a social life equally
regenerative and fleeting. [...] Voice, image, metaphor,
symbol, metrical organization, traditional form—all the
accouterments of poetic discourse are temporalized and
hence located within a context that forces them to signify.
[...] we are reading a scene of reading and we are in it."[12]

This recursiveness becomes more pronounced in De
Angelis's fourth and most recent collection, *Distante un*

padre (*A Distant Father*, 1989). The poems are filled with
memories of the poet's relationships to family and friends.
The extreme formal discontinuity makes the memories
obscure, impersonalizing them to the point of inscrutabil-
ity, but the poems remain forcefully resonant, shot through
with De Angelis's recurrent ideas and images, occasion-
ally quoting and revising lines from other of his poems,
forcing the reader to confront the changing conditions of
language and subjectivity. "Telegram" is typically allusive.
Its reference to "symbols for the dead" echoes De Angelis's
"The Sentries" from *Resemblances*, which mentions those
who "withdraw from death to escort it" with "second-hand
symbols." But "Telegram" also reworks Celan's range of
meanings for blue by deploying the color to represent the
origins of the poem, the Muse of otherness to whom the
poet listens, isolated by his estranging use of language,
already one of "the masters of ice and of stone." For De
Angelis, language has a dual aspect: on the one hand, it
transforms what it describes, imposing a conceptual sys-
tem like mathematics ("a few square meters"), empower-
ing a technology ("a drill, scarcely out"); on the other hand,
it brings awareness of the transformation, of the differ-
ence that exceeds linguistic determination, likened here
to a parting and death, but also to "the first moments of a
thing." This is an originary "intuition" that takes thinking
back to biology, to nature, but via mythology, Demeter
anxiously awaiting the rebirth of a "daughter," Proserpine
"breathing" at the abyss of becoming. De Angelis's poem
is a "telegram" from the edge of language, received in stac-
cato bursts of lines, where the opaque details seem by turns
realistic, autobiographical, figurative, multiplying mean-
ings by interrupting signification.

     The postmodern concerns of De Angelis's poetic project

give it an international currency, but it also bears a re-
semblance to those of other Italian poets who began to
publish during the 1970s, poets like Nanni Cagnone,
Angelo Lumelli, and Giuseppe Conte. Thomas Harrison
has described the basic outline of this project: "the poet
sings Dionysos—not in the hope of recalling the gods," as
Heidegger's pursuit of being encourages, "but to celebrate
their absence," following Nietzsche and poststructuralist
thinkers like Gilles Deleuze who have commented on and
developed his antimetaphysical philosophy.[13] What makes
De Angelis different from other experimentalists in Italy
is that his philosophical explorations coincide with his rig-
orous development of an originary poetics and a unique
repertoire of images and scenes, partly literary and partly
autobiographical in provenance. The discontinuous form
of his poetry clearly derives from both the neoavantgarde
and hermeticism. Yet he avoids the explicit political en-
gagement of the former and the controlled ambiguity of
the latter and rather fosters an indeterminacy of meaning
that may well be even more radical in its political implica-
tions: its aim is to recall the unstable origins of language
and subjectivity, of culture and society. The undeniable
power of De Angelis's writing has already distinguished
him as one of the most compelling figures in post-WWII
Italian poetry.

*

For the English-language translator, however, there is
still the question of how De Angelis's writing can be made
just as compelling in English—the question, that is, of
developing a translation strategy. After working with his
writing for more than fifteen years, I have come to feel

that an appropriate strategy must take into account the considerable differences between Italian and Anglo-American culture. For much of this century, British and American philosophy has been dominated by the analytical tradition, which tends to privilege intentionality and reference in the study of language and therefore has had little patience with the critique of subjectivity and representation in Continental movements like phenomenology. During the same period, philosophical thinking has remained alien to most poetry in Britain and the United States. In a polemical essay published in 1967, Kenneth Rexroth wondered, "Why Is American Poetry Culturally Deprived?" because he "never met an American poet who was familiar with Jean Paul Sartre's attempts at philosophy, much less with the gnarled discourse of Scheler or Heidegger."[14] Rexroth's point, which he felt also applied to British poetry, continues to be true some twenty-five years later. Among the noteworthy exceptions today are the diverse group of so-called "L=A=N=G=U=A=G=E" writers, such as Charles Bernstein, who has eroded the generic distinction between poetry and essay by drawing on various European traditions and thinkers, including Dada and Surrealism, Brecht and the Frankfurt School, Wittgenstein and poststructuralism.[15] Since Bernstein's aesthetic has earned his writing a marginal position in American publishing, banished to the relative obscurity of the small press and the little magazine, it suggests that contemporary American culture is not likely to give an enthusiastic reception to a poet like De Angelis, who writes with a knowledge of the main currents in Continental philosophy. De Angelis enjoys a much more central position in Italian culture: his writing is published by both small and large presses and reviewed by noted critics in a

wide range of newspapers and magazines, both local and
national, little and mass-audience.

Perhaps what most complicates De Angelis's reception
in English is that his texts run counter to the aesthetic
that has dominated Anglo-American poetry from
Wordsworth to T. S. Eliot to Robert Lowell and beyond.
This is transparency, the view, as Antony Easthope puts
it, that "poetry expresses experience; experience gives ac-
cess to personality, and so poetry leads us to personality."[16]
The "experience" and "personality" are of course the poet's:
transparency is an individualistic aesthetic based on the
assumption that a poem is the consciously controlled ex-
pression of the poet's psychology or intention. Yet trans-
parency is in fact an illusionism: it happens only when the
poet has evoked a coherent speaking voice by producing
a text with specific formal elements, like consistent pro-
nouns, linear syntax, univocal meaning. De Angelis's texts
can serve as a negative confirmation of this point because
they issue a decisive challenge to transparency. In using
thinkers like Nietzsche, Heidegger, and Lacan, he implic-
itly rejects the individualistic conception of human con-
sciousness assumed in transparent discourse: his poetry
represents the subject not as the unified source of mean-
ing, freely expressing its experience in language, but as
determined and divided by its changing and often unac-
knowledged conditions. And this rejection of individual-
ism coincides with an abandonment of the formal tech-
niques used to achieve transparency. De Angelis's texts
do not offer the reader a clearly defined position from
which to understand them, or a psychologically stable
voice with which to identify. On the contrary, their shift-
ing, anonymous voices, abrupt line-breaks, and frag-
mented syntax constantly disrupt the signifying process,

requiring the reader to reconsider interpretations. The result of this formal discontinuity is that it fails to generate the illusionistic effect of authorial presence, demonstrating, with degrees of discomfort that vary with readers' aesthetic preferences, how much transparency depends on the materiality of language. To be sure, De Angelis does not pursue anything like the extreme linguistic experiments of such L=A=N=G=U=A=G=E writers as Bernstein, particularly the cultivation of syntactical ambiguity and the foregrounding of sound over sense. Still, the discontinuity, opacity, and anti-individualism of De Angelis's texts align them more closely to such experiments than to the transparency that continues to dominate Anglo-American poetry.

The English-language translator can only regard this domination as questionable because it has made fluency the sole strategy to gain wide acceptance in poetry translation. A fluent strategy creates the appearance that the target-language text reflects the foreign poet's personality or intention or the essential meaning of the source-language text. Once again, however, this is an illusionism which depends on the translator's sometimes laborious manipulation of language. In order to read fluently, a translation must not contain any awkward phrasings, unidiomatic constructions, or confused meanings. When the poem to be translated is in free verse, varied rhythms that avoid jogtrot meters are needed to give the language a conversational quality, to make it sound natural. Line-breaks should not distort the syntax so much as to frustrate the search for intelligibility; they should rather support the syntactical continuity that gets the reader to read for meaning over the lines, pursuing the evocation of a voice, tracing its psychological contours. Although trans-

parency depends on the translator's implementation of
these formal techniques, it conceals the work, even the very
presence of language (let alone the fact that two languages
are involved), by suggesting that the foreign poet can be
seen in the translated text, that in it he speaks in his own
voice.

Here the crucial problem confronting the English-lan-
guage translator of De Angelis's poetry comes more clearly
into focus: since his texts abandon transparency, they make
the adoption of a fluent translation strategy very difficult,
if not simply impossible. How, then, should they be trans-
lated into English? A translator could certainly genuflect
to the prevailing cult of the author and produce a transla-
tion that imposes fluency on De Angelis's poetry. A rigor-
ous application of this strategy would involve minimizing
the syntactical fragmentation, for example, by inserting
subjects and verbs to create complete sentences. Thus, the
eleventh line of "The Central Idea" might read "were hiss-
ing" instead of merely "hissing," and the second line of "The
Dream of the Dancing Cat" might read "there are roads"
instead of merely "roads." Some effort could also be made
to distinguish between the anonymous voices in De
Angelis's poetry by developing a unique tone and diction
for each of the quoted statements, fashioning them into a
comprehensible dialogue. Such techniques would of course
do little to alter the elliptical, densely metaphoric quality
of so many of his poems and therefore would not achieve
the high level of fluency necessary for transparent dis-
course.

But I have taken another tack. My translation refuses
fluency and rather seeks to reproduce the formal disconti-
nuity that characterizes De Angelis's Italian texts. This
has meant adhering closely to their syntactical irregulari-

ties, using similar departures from English wherever the
poet has evidently departed from standard Italian usage.
In some cases, I have even omitted subjects and verbs,
withstanding the tendency of English to make these forms
explicit wherever a Romance language like Italian allows
them to remain implicit. Similarly, my translation follows
the line-breaks in the Italian and occasionally resorts to
an English word that heightens their abruptness, their
effect of throwing the reading process off balance and forc-
ing the reader to revise expectations. I have also tried to
recreate the polysemy of De Angelis's poetry by translat-
ing some phrases quite literally, risking obscurity but open-
ing up a range of meanings that would be limited by a
freer, more idiomatic rendering.

My strategy, taking its cue from De Angelis's own aes-
thetic of discontinuity, can be called resistancy. And imple-
menting this strategy does manage to preserve the pecu-
liarities of De Angelis's poetry in English—but only to
certain extent. It should not be viewed as necessarily mak-
ing the translations more faithful to the Italian texts. Al-
though resistancy can be said to rest on the same basic
assumptions about language and subjectivity that inform
De Angelis's poetry, my English version nonetheless de-
viates from the Italian, qualifying its meaning with addi-
tions and subtractions even in those places where I tried
to be most faithful. In "The Sounds That Arrived," for
instance, I used "schoolmistress" to translate "maestra,"
the feminine form of "teacher." The English word succeeds
in communicating the gender, but because it is now virtu-
ally obsolete in English, it not only misses the simplicity
and directness of the rather common Italian word, but
introduces an archaic note which is completely absent from
De Angelis's poem. All the same, the choice of "school-

mistress" leads to a different kind of fidelity: the archaism makes for a slightly more discontinuous translation by increasing its linguistic diversity and inscribes in its very diction the chronological reversal figured in the imagery, the backward movement through childhood to the moment of conception.

This example shows that resistancy, like any translation strategy, enables a translation to do no more than approximate a foreign text. In contrast to fluency, however, a resistant strategy does not conceal the fact that the translation it makes possible is actually a translation, not to be confused with the text produced by the foreign writer. A resistant translation in English proves especially effective in avoiding this mystifying concealment: since it is based on formal discontinuity, it implicitly challenges the transparent aesthetic that, in its domination of Anglo-American poetry and poetry translation, would attempt to domesticate even the most discontinuous foreign writing by recommending a fluent strategy. Using resistancy to translate De Angelis's poetry, therefore, can prevent any such domestication and maintain its foreignness in English by resorting to analogous techniques of fragmentation and proliferation of meaning. The archaic word in "The Sounds That Arrived" makes the translation more unusual and distancing to the English-language reader by drawing attention to itself as a word and thus abusing the canon of transparency.

Such points of textual energy can be understood as conforming to an ethics of translation, an effort to preserve the difference of the foreign text. They are comparable to what Emmanuel Levinas calls the "trace" of another person, the addressee in any act of communication. "The trace," Levinas states, "is the presence of whoever, strictly

speaking, has never been there" because this person could
only appear in a mediated form, through the self's repre-
sentation; "the trace establishes a personal and ethical re-
lation" with the other by "signifying something without
causing it to appear."[17] For Levinas, the trace of the other
is best exemplified by unique facial features, by what
makes him or her strange and cannot be encompassed by
the self's discourse. For the reader of a resistant transla-
tion, the points of textual energy constitute the trace of
the foreign text, a cultural other which is always already
absent because replaced by the target language; and this
trace allows the reader to experience, however briefly, the
irreducible differences that separate two languages, two
texts, two cultures. It is this sort of estranging experience
that my translation of De Angelis's poetry aims to pro-
vide for the English-language reader.

*

Many years in the making, this translation has incurred
a number of debts which I would here like to acknowl-
edge. The first and greatest of these is to Milo De Angelis,
not only for writing such remarkable texts, but also for
responding patiently to my myriad questions about them
over the years. I am grateful to Douglas Messerli for his
adventurous decision to publish the translation and for
suggesting the provocative title. Ruth Feldman and Brian
Swann initially got me to translate some of De Angelis's
poems for an anthology they were editing, and I profited
from their criticisms of my first, tentative efforts. Stephen
Sartarelli read most of the translations against the Italian
texts with his customary care and made many helpful cor-
rections and recommendations. Jonathan Galassi gave his

encouraging support to this project from the very begin-
ning and offered some invaluable advice. Special thanks
are also due to Rachel Du Plessis and Susan Stewart, for
their incisive comments on an early version of the intro-
duction; to Charles Bardes, for guiding me through Paul
Celan's "Schliere"; to Michael Henry Heim, for helping
with some Czech references; to Carla Weinberg, for gen-
erously preparing a transcription of interviews with the
poet; and to Harry Mathews, for suggesting some variant
readings. The lines in the dedication appear in Celan's
poem "Miterhoben" from *Schneepart* (Frankfurt:
Suhrkamp, 1971).

L. V.

New York City

August 1993

Notes

1 Giuseppe Conte, "Le istituzioni del desidero," *Il Verri*, 2 (September 1976):
  53–76 (68). All English translations of Italian writing are mine.
2 *I Novissimi: poesie per gli anni '60*, ed. Alfredo Giuliani (Milan: Rusconi
  e Paolazzi, 1961), p. xviii.
3 Franco Fortini, "The Wind of Revival," *The Times Literary Supplement*,
  31 October 1975, pp. 1308–9.
4 Edoardo Sanguineti, "Purgatorio de l'Inferno," *Triperuno* (Milan:
  Feltrinelli, 1964), pp. 69–88.
5 Martin Heidegger, *Being and Time*, trans. John Macquarrie and Ed-
  ward Robinson (New York: Harper and Row, 1962), especially pp. 219–
  24.
6 Friedrich Nietzsche, *The Will to Power*, trans. and ed. Walter Kaufmann
  and R. J. Hollingdale (New York: Random House, 1967), p. 331.
7 See, for example, Jacques Lacan, "The Subversion of the Subject and
  the Dialectic of Desire in the Freudian Unconscious," *Ecrits: A Selec-
  tion*, trans. Alan Sheridan (New York: Norton, 1977), pp. 292–325.

8 Nietzsche, *The Birth of Tragedy*, trans. and ed. Walter Kaufmann (New York: Random House, 1967), p. 71.

9 George Mylonas, *Eleusis and the Eleusinian Mysteries* (Princeton: Princeton University Press, 1961), p. 228.

10 Paul Celan, "The Meridian," *Collected Prose*, trans. Rosmarie Waldrop (Manchester: Carcanet, 1986), pp. 37–55 (48).

11 *Paul Celan: Poems*, ed. and trans. Michael Hamburger (New York: Persea, 1980), p. 87.

12 Susan Stewart, "The Last Man," *American Poetry Review*, September/October 1988, pp. 9–16 (9, 11).

13 Thomas J. Harrison, ed. and trans., *The Favorite Malice: Ontology and Reference in Contemporary Italian Poetry* (New York, Norristown, and Milan: Out of London, 1983), p. 40.

14 Kenneth Rexroth, "Why Is American Poetry Culturally Deprived?" (1967), rpt. in *TriQuarterly* 20, 63 (1985): 53–59 (57).

15 See Charles Bernstein, *Content's Dream: Essays 1975–1984* (Los Angeles: Sun and Moon Press, 1986). For a selection from the writing of the loosely associated "L=A=N=G=U=A=G=E" group, see *"Language" Poetries: An Anthology*, ed. Douglas Messerli (New York: New Directions, 1987). The British poet Tom Raworth is in many ways comparable to these American writers in his deviation from the dominant aesthetic in Anglo–American poetry: see his book *Tottering State: Selected and New Poems 1963–1983* (Great Barrington, MA: The Figures, 1984).

16 Antony Easthope, *Poetry as Discourse* (London and New York: Methuen, 1983), pp. 4–5.

17 Emmanuel Levinas, "On the Trail of the Other," trans. Daniel J. Hoy, *Philosophy Today*, 10 (1966): 34–45 (44, 45).

I

RESEMBLANCES

The Central Idea

came to mind (but by chance, because of the scent
of alcohol and the bandages)
this careful busying of oneself
notwithstanding.
And still, in front of everybody, there was choosing
between the actions and their meaning.
But by chance.
Despotic beings made a gift of the center
absentmindedly, with an x-ray,
and in a dream threatening bosses
hissing:
"if we take from you what isn't yours,
you'll have nothing left."

He Who Has Dared

He who—back to the wall—
becomes true
knows, seriously, "knows"
like these fields: only after the bonfires
do they become real and finite, or this stable pathetic
and yet it is politic
to k n o w

but when others more alive
dart downhill, winning,
one shouts that, yes, the first time
isn't the most profound
but he wanted it…

                   and he knew well

to descend truly
without guile means cutting off
the way back.
But completely?
And does shifting the order of the factors
change it or not?

Now

This desired caress, stopped
close by, will not reach the cheek, gossip
that holds no truth: better
the Nazi gesture that crushes his mind, mine.
Not comprehended
it will comprehend everything
with the struggle in the room, the imploring
look and then:
listen to me
it helps. The day escaped into the day after
to forget. Now
in a few awkward tears
it is put before you: you are contemporary.

Only

Only this growing
indifferent to the glance and full
of what was seen
was possible: if there are
two boats
it isn't their meeting point that mattered, but the beauty
of the journey in the water: only this way,
only now, don't explain.
And it's cruel
but you must say no to his face that
weeps and doesn't understand, and loves
as people have loved for millennia, vowing
to a dark balcony, stroking themselves
among the threatening leaves.

The Island

The face too, on waking
every time, panic and anxiety
of becoming different:
an entire century flew by
in its movements
because it was uniqueness.
And yet someone, already safe,
challenging suicides near the bed and pills
dropped from hands
someone is saying:
the island will be observed in its beauty
whether by us or others doesn't matter.

A Loser

Outside is history,
the struggling classes.
What can you do once and for all
rejecting the world
accepting it in the morning
("It was true, you know, the quarrel with her
was serious. But there was only one bed
and our bodies prevailed.").
There were biological
limits and great laws of profit.
So gods and the interior were invented.
At night, during his erection,
he even laid claim to fate
("where've you been
all my life?").

Metaphors

The same low sky
of ambulances and rain, in the excitement
and hands on the groin, summoned by the body
to oppose
the slightest numbness to things
while outside, among the traffic lights, Europe
having invented the finite
holds out
far from the beast, defends
real and irrelevant concepts
along the highways, in linear time
toward a point
and the eyes don't shut before things, steady
where today a millenium hesitated
between yielding and not yielding
losing itself always later, with intelligence.

There Is No Reason

There is no reason to do it
or not to do it
as when you lived
sharing meals and the dishonesty
of planning
                and now
in the dense weave
of what happens, with
methedrine
there's a need determined but undirected
near the body
now it's certain:
you improve only in a small way, in an infinitely
small way, six hours
here, the closest possible, knowing the contrary
is also true.

The Sentries

Doing the deed where the river is deep
not even like this, with hypnotics
and panic, can something be shown
to others who never saw it
during their own, distant, and this night
which they are watching

in a borrowed language,
without a single imperative action,
they hold themselves back
with words, second-hand symbols,

they speak but without revealing the origin
they made of elsewhere an inhabitable temple
in the shadow along the ravines
they withdraw from death to escort it.

The Resemblance

He was
in the villages, walking hurriedly
that one absolutely
beyond
who issued from books into history
skimming the stalls in summer.
We'll beg his pardon
for having tried, in the stadium,
asking him to hurl the javelin
so he might restore childhood.
You can't
but the resemblance was ours
in another's image, close at hand, in the sunlight
we wanted to restrain our feelings
toward him
in a revivifying gesture: who could confirm
that everything was on this side?

He began to run, held out his arm...

Becoming

Another action, in the vineyard, gathering
this dusty, sweet muscatel
among the ants
that run across the sweat
on your back, hurrying
beneath a sun that dries up everything
while the plain broadens, and something
that was enormous disappears
slips from the terror to the uneasiness
of becoming indifferent, until the last
tremor, nothing.

Gee

A child pointed at the sky, made it his,
and then he points at the one he loves
and it's his sky, immediately

because if he doesn't seize it's beyond love
beyond the living, humble hand
which knows, recognizes its theft
but doesn't ask forgiveness, and loves:

he beautifies nothing, doesn't expect
act after act, more and more here
near his wool, his sweater...

and now, on the sand,
in the human circle round the clothes
the water that invites swimming
doesn't wait, isn't old
and finally the tender gesture
that one receives in the waves
isn't just for him.

The Window

In the hotel
room, behind the curtains
revealing for the first time
a fond square
"I would like only to repeat, you understand, nothing else"
this afternoon
it's impersonal, doesn't apply to anyone
doesn't select, is already a land
full of guests, who complete
its started work
in someone else
as that bridge stays there
calm, no longer
uniting two banks.

The First Comes

"Oh if you only knew:
anyone who suffers
anyone who suffers isn't profound."
Suburbs of Turin. Summer. By now
there isn't much water in the river, the newsstand is closed.
"Change, don't wait any longer."
There are only a few cars near the wall.
No one goes by. We remain sitting
on the parapet. "Maybe you can still
become a loner, can
still feel without paying, can enter
into a depth that isn't
commemorative: don't wait for anyone,
don't wait for me, if I suffer, don't wait for me."
And we stare at the dark water, this slight breeze
stirring it
into thin veins, like wood.
It touches my face.
"When will you break away, when will you have no
alternatives? Don't cling, accept
accept
losing something."

The Train Corridor

"Again this plagiary
of resemblance—do you want this?" in the cold train
that crosses the rice fields and separates everything
"you want this, you think this
is love?" It is dark now
and the deserted corridor lengthens
while the elbows, leaning on the compartment window
"you're still there,
but it's time to change expectations" and a station
passes, in the fog, its opaque houses.
"But what plagiary? If I believe
in something, then it will be true for you too,
truer than your world, I confute it always"
a trembling
beneath the overcoat, the body follows a force
that conquers, leans the word against itself
"something, listen,
something can begin."

Anywhere Except

He talks to someone

and he answers, it's something different but
he answers: no one would forgive him
if he comes back ice, the being identical to himself
who doesn't walk.

He answers, answers

He's inside, he must continue, at an infinite
rate, like a word
discovered with other words
he must talk, must bathe in a river
that isn't his but keeps him alive, and has no banks.

And on this country road
the girl removes her sweater, lowers the seat
and doesn't know whether they are two, three, or she is alone
but she continues, feels the dampness, moves her muscles

"please stay inside me"
  "are you sure?"
    "yes, I want you inside, I love you."

Stones in the Warm Mud

Laugh once, when the evening
wind carries a wonder
that can't be seen, but resumes
in the outline of the shadows and profanes the pact
and sees the crabapple, the poplar
birds whose meaning and need
to be born again are unknown
yet in the air they carved out a right
direction, the liberating
current, in the ocean, the same one
that now conquers the moment
oaks and poplars
of the woman warrior who is sleeping
in the warmth of an esteem
denser toward the end: already the trapped fly
frees itself in flight
melody of the water and the conch
which a gesture will change into experience,
within a complete action, suddenly
after escaping among the branches

here's the dusty road, the field
salvation
swimming toward a luminous calm
shelter for the hares
tired of traps, after millennia,
and the storm, the clearing sky
everything is so alone
it can become anything.

The Slowness

"I used to want everything to stop"
she says
her scarf tied tightly
as we walk through the puddles
"I didn't want to become different"
and the words are confused, between the steps, today,
at the edge of the sidewalk
"Jezkova is faraway
and I never know about the others" and meanwhile
this countryside begins, at the end of the street
the scent of courtyards
after the last buses "...what joy...what
are you talking about...is this enough for you...
this love full of duties...where
at best one is forgiven...those who can be...
you're content with this..."
but there's too much wind, and words full of consonants
to say that it's ending
and we syllabify "*nerozumím, nerozumím*"
in the morning pale as her blonde hair

an elusive thing
sliding over the asphalt, only once
"…but now the evidence is for us…
we who can't see…" the trucks
pass by slowly, loaded,
at the end of the turn
and the walls of these houses, the kitchen odors
"where are you" she asks me, in an undemonstrable
language, and does not speak.

The Causes of the Beginning

There was a solar interval
and a warm yellow over the leaves
and then the birth
of the byzantine smile

> *but you can't "seek"*
> *the metamorphosis*
> *make an unprepared gesture*
> *no one can say*
> *what he loved the first time*

the slender body, moved by the wind,
crosses a street
it is granted flowers, the rippling grass
and the dream of the princess
in the room, the sweet certainty
of not being
visible

it's incredible, you still believed in the center
of matter
and you wept because it's only yours
and you wanted to say, to say
but there's no more time to make the instant

and a delicate sweat on the neck
means "yes"
as the festive wind
slowly removes the tunic
without a gesture
and the spirits of air and water,
the scent of the river, the shout

advancing in the distance
a body can also be found, at the edge,
how many times has it happened
within these complicated orders
in the world revealed
to anyone who turns to the other side

the hill is covered
with vineyards, while everything has a right time
and the steps over the clods are slow
for the sake of the joy

only what comes out first counts
and now bad luck doesn't defeat chance,
it's always too late to be precise
so say it anyway, say you're living, say it.

Noon Glare

What a strange smile
lives to be here and not to be right
in this square
he who confides and he who consoles are suddenly silent
it's June, in broad daylight the embrace comes
not tomorrow, now

the afternoon, the reflections
on the restaurant tables
near the red fingernails
give no explanations
they match the talk
this is the caress

that forgets and dedicates
while he looks inside the coffee cup
at the remaining drops and thinks of the time
and his only word of love: "now."

"A.S."

I

All of you no doubt have felt
the soft sleep, the sweetest dizziness
easing you down on the bed
and then the tree, the bark, the algae,
the eyes don't turn away
and the vials are no longer threatening
in the chiaroscuro of the afternoon
as a thousand animals
surround the stretcher, block the nurses
the labored breathing more and more shallow
in the frosted windows
of the ambulance, the windowsill of a floor
appears, the interval
that releases the living
and sets them racing with the current in the pupils,
sparkling at the moment of the offer.
And suddenly, the quiet
of the vineyard and the well, the smooth stone

tearing the flesh
a calm deep within the grain
as the woman on the field gives birth
more and more slowly,
until the son returns in the fecundation
and earlier still, in the kiss, in the glimmer
of a room, the large mirror,
growing desire, the gesture.

II

And then you have also felt, at least once
when the liquid issues most delicately
from the lips, flows yellow in the washbasin
the probe and the sirens ever more distant.
The breathing subsides, stops, resumes
how peaceful is the beach frozen by the storm:
a canoe drifts toward a coral island
and beneath the sea sexual cells couple
there are no irreparable events
only the cyclic sponges, the insects
that blanket the air:
look, mother-of-pearl, a rock in the sand,
footprints, look, manna,
the bathrobe he removes with a single gesture

the solemnity of the light, the wonder, the first
and the female pelican
calls her brood scattered in the storm
and perhaps sees something, among the reefs,
something that moves
tomorrow she will run with her children,
mingled among them, to breathe
in the deep turquoise of the tide
rising to the surface, reviving now
and finding a different land, another voice.

The Sounds That Arrived

The wolf is still under the blanket
and a thousand questions are needed to grasp it
even if the desire
is to believe in everything at once
uttering a quiet, intense thanks
the unity of the sand, the right hand touching
the luminous left on the Egyptian statues
a calm that remains,
blooms again in the rite, this June
it's an answered prayer
the schoolmistress, the little stairs
the hair color is in the womb
and then the golden instant,
the lemon's dark green.

The Dream of the Dancing Cat

For the lady of sea and grain
roads
without beginnings, bright clothes, leavened bread
because she spoke
as if she never existed,
in the plain
of light or in the threatening hiss
of the reeds, spoke
without need of guarantees,
swift shadow on the horse
heading south, beyond the forest, tonight.

Form

The mystery of what another man
sees
at the fall of a dress
separates sense
from the name "stefania."

Assassins

Where the move
to be here demands an undiscoverable
choice, sacred wait, season:
the shadows, in the listening,
at the edges of the face
stop in the solemnity
dividing dagger
from act.

Neither Point Nor Line

Like the drop, on the leaf, after the storm
only for the second time

he never knew anyone
because he wanted to be precise
till death

light zen, in the field,
the force that held the birds in flight
(an interruption and they would fall)
becomes the hell of counting them.

And Then the Water

In the harvest too
the body was only lent
because it wanted to become
innocent in the end

and running
it didn't renounce
an anthology of gestures

the slender body
entering the princess's room
to love the first time.

II

MILLIMETERS

The canes

The canes
have smashed the last bucket
and now the village grows
silent
in the court martial. Here
is the ink, amid a multitude
thirsty on schedule,
a surname:
all the soft eggs
will arrive
perforce or disdainfully
and that
pharaoh will give the lash
which still wounds today
and makes them earthly.
The one who breeds time
wears a furrowed face and patiently repeats
that we obey.

Now she is unadorned

Now she is unadorned
and the years come to pass, in handfuls,
with the wit of shears and
an arrogance that draws
to the gas the mouth
persistent down to the spine
where it believes
or else the dead trudge toward a field
with a hollow head
and the myriads
hurl themselves into the baptism
for a breath.

Born on the earth

Born on the earth
that remains
we were that breathless rejoicing
as soon as the minds arrived
on a canary's back
and conquered. A
matron-at-arms
is screwed to our flank, guardian
of the tablets, a harpoon
in the Mediterranean world, among the eggs.

You didn't want to share
the plunder and so
you have me forever
because there was nothing else
but the mere victory. Later
we shall throw our prey
to the cats: they will know
how to annihilate it!

Here is the quartz page
in the agenda, when
every man is razed to the ground
and remembers. The pine cones fill
this courtyard
faithful to its meters: the very tree
of the door
that is perennial for anyone who notices it
and yet is air, only air. It has a severity
and a still attentive custodian. These
were the numbers.

For you who

For you who
mute this voice
the ears arrive, terribly fast,
and they all have a cheap
neck beneath the shears,
a benediction just for them;
for them and the universe. Solemn,
shattered in every muscle,
they hurl the tractor, the enormous triangle
where August is camped
and lives on figs
and everyone is prey,
clenched down to their own iron: a
tropical calm, a vigil.

The drop ready for the globe

The drop ready for the globe
and the most unfamiliar
names of chance
finally reached a short cut
with a few strokes of the file
supported the glass
on one finger, brother
of the first time. The entire
field, with its
buried bicycles, squeezes out
words like a ventriloquist:
half to the victory, half
to the grass in the trap.

In us the universe will arrive,
that head-on silence where we
have already been.

There is a hand that nails

There is a hand that nails
its grams
in the courtyard near Greece
the numbers
are increasingly chaste
city of cotton and bronze
and the summer with a mouth facing north.
Here pass the bodies
we surprise, females
proud in quarrels. Or
they are silent;
or shadows, challenges, snares. The stones
know them well.

It's always them,
always them, like birthdays. Now
a storm returns
along the spinal column and they select
the spell and the incursion,
a shrug of the shoulders or a nakedness.

The voice that proclaimed herself
twin and sphere and teeth of twins
darts into her mountain
with the same life
sworn immediately, before dawn. They gave her
an almond
without a gunsight or space. But
she decided at once, she fired!

Yes, that was
the circle of foreigners
with inordinate pride, who rave
about a pact...I was there...look closely...I was already there...
storm and dirge of the woman
who bears a son in her womb and one ascending
in my ancient place
you arrive
minds full of light
with the roar of a lottery drawing
every paradise is dizzy
with sons mown and certain.

July arrives for the dead

July arrives for the dead
who feel in the siege
of every flower
a remote justice. And a
paper noose
is reborn relentlessly
in the history
of the earth, vast, precipitous,
numberless things, clothes white and worm-eaten,
farm-workers hidden
in the wheat. Or still
farther within, wherever the chrysanthemums
scream. Shuttling
between the walls of the head and
a long-distance call, this minute
is counted;
and the urn—it too a delight
of the mixed magnanimous ones—
has said enough.

A teacher

A teacher
swam in the dawn
of things, between five-forty
and good luck

>   "we shall learn
>   how to eat this onion,
>   bit by bit, observing the silence
>   of each taste"

and the pupils who are dead in time
now drink
a cup of warm milk

but you found us

and you chose in the cat
those meows that
don't do it on purpose!

You can't be silent

You can't be silent
on this mountain
we will come ploughed
in peace and among the birds.
The whiteness flies away and those teeth
know, thread grasped
by the eternally plural
when
they declare us true: they didn't fall,
not even then, they held
the sun in the second, in the third throat.
This was the winter
thrown
with an ancient newspaper, brother. In
a lit basket
it dies and gushes
from there, from the mesh.
And I speak of the earth
to a candle;
of you and of us, of us alone, created.

III

LAND OF THE FACE

Letter from Vignole

We heard the rain and those
who were returning: each thing
in the calm of speaking
and then the mountain, an instant, and all
the dead whom not even your exile
can distinguish.

"Come back at once or don't ever come back."

This—amid the psalms
of the law—was the voice
that you repeated at the beginning,
the potent syllable, before
you yourself.

"Only then shall I come to meet you, unaware
in the winter which I lost and find."

In History

As one hears stone, like
you, the winters. Silence. The squad
is passing by, one man at a time. You who
carry out the execution
you, slain and
dodging. Listening
to the howl, the sleeping amphora, when it
cracked...descend, touch the cottages,
the rare joy
of paradise and the entire slope
fills
with hemlock still green
as goldfinches expose
the bones
in the rustling of our
death. With shoulders
that used to fight, covered with dust, he will mow
the precipice. He will be
valorous. Don't hesitate. Like stitches of
light, everyone rejoices
at a supper turned blue, once.

No One, Yet They Return

I

At the back of the crawlspace lie animal bones,
touched one at a time. We awake
on a stool and know with certainty
we're alive: this mouth remains in pandemonium,
this hollow season of carnival pins
and the rush of pain, while the elevators
carry on, like litanies. It's raining hard.
The entire squad runs wild
from one bakery to the next, shelled by stones.

II

Waiting for the hailstorm that an entire century
promised your children, then hurling them on the
sidewalk with a slap at the throat, when the asphalt
is strewn with radiation and the porter's room is locked.
They are women, they approach cleaving the air,
dressed like Indians. There's no time to reflect
in this hissing. It's as if everything were happening

in enormous quantities. I don't even know
what bodies I'll have to stop: but this time
doesn't miss a step and one by one descends
where they cried out.

Ronefor

A shove, a cavity of flesh or air
which by chance—always finds me
here at Sesto, in its stench and in
its essential form. No one
will know how to stain the salvation
of this India, my obsession:
it isn't a veil or a mantra, certainly, I've already
gone kilometers north, I already know
I will die on the outskirts, with mineral intelligence
and a fee to be silent: *but what
I suffered wasn't me*, nor does the darkened summit
bridle the wayfarers' dash to civilization.
Vomit and sky, when they meet,
astonishing, in us. That time
I looked closely. Minute infamies, the great styles
of industry, the gas of the afternoon...it was
the same attention to disaster
and the missing money, with hands
pried open and shoulders in the nothing, in the house,
in the hour known by everyone, that
precise dialect, when it states
my probabilities and doesn't look at me.

Via Prospero Finzi

"And they will all arrive
because the time that leads nowhere
has already been suspended.

You see, a few years
in front of me, a sort
of prohibited death: leave me,
you know I won't fall.

There's a memory,
a burst of laughter in which I change or stop.

In this crowd
of the semiconscious and ferry-bodies
the pill mixes
with the blood; and we descend.

But colorless, colorless.

On the return trip, God won't find
even an error to resolve.
I look at the wall
against which you lean, tremble, laugh.
I too was born there."

In the Lungs

The blanket, its weight, while we were growing.
Or the eyes, which yesterday were blind,
today yours, yesterday the indivisible. The vials,
the boiled rice becomes the only
world without symbol. Matter that
was only matter, nothing that
was only matter. Watch, don't watch, poetry,
cobalt, father, nothing, poplars.

Conversation with Father

I

The prisoners, you said, found
an opening in the cell. Several
died frostbitten, in the night.
Others, however, by burning their clothes,
saved themselves. But why was the guard
silent? Is it true he shot only at the dead?

II

The bandage was riddled with holes
but it didn't fall from his eyes. The blinds
were nearly closed...I'm certain...they were nearly closed
and no one can forgive them
not even now, among the other windows,
parcels from the post office. This truck. Now
it's dark. It was
as if he heard

a sister devoured, before him, lead
and light...I think so...she was watching,
she was strange...German.
The clock was stolen, at once, and then
filth on top of filth, cats
pelted with stones,
they too, like an anecdote of the crowd.

I Recover a Syntax

I recover a syntax in centuries already studied
dismissing both the east and the clouds.
Molding the dream with what the idea embraces is hard.
No one will violate an inherited dream.

Here the loud, childlike races urged by it
freeze in the chest. Sometimes I can fix
my eyes on the street signs, on the
precise force of impact, which restores
to that theater its fear of death.

Talking to Dario

"The carpet will give
at a precise point
I don't know which
I think
that it will be cold there, that
my step will collapse
during a season
I button my overcoat,
my gray face."

"I could act as background. I could
touch things.
This city, you said,
has always understood us.
And even later, tottering
on the edge of the tub
or recalling a fish sealed
in a plastic bag. No,
we won't be surreal. You shall die
pointing at it—your breath."

"Just look at it, look:
don't separate the two realms. Neither the one
you imagine, nor
the one you'll
see. The animals
brush against me. To turn back
into an unanimous thing,
the blood is here. We could
touch our overcoats or blind ourselves.
They are all our
acts of justice."

The Killing

Someone hesitated before the light-switch,
but then he struck all the same because of a buzzing
of days in the kitchen
again and always an elegy of herds
which the poison nonetheless distinguishes.

This, with its quiet style, was hatred
and the thousand atoms in the artery that awaited
the killing that wasn't rapid or doubtful or anything,
but a pure killing without footprints:
in a spring whiteness the body stirred.

And so the story continues and you have a suspicion
of another time: millennia
encrusted in the resin, people
who fill the skin, the garbage can, the nightmare
of hands, when sleep
abandons them near the ditch.

Foreweb

There is a crime
I don't know whether committed or witnessed
in a styleless time, like a breeze
blue and darkling, which moved
the right hand. Or someone
who, bitten by caries, screams.
Then even the dust mote makes
unquestionable flights and even
a knee hurt in the corner kick
stitches male back to female.

Will You Put on the Blindfold?

Will you put on the blindfold? I climbed with my scarf
over my eyes, I scratched the bricks. The wall
has many cracks, but don't be afraid, you mustn't be afraid:
you'll climb up the creepers, the creeping brothers.

It's very high up here. Put on the blindfold? I climbed
in a few minutes, look, my nails are bloody,
I'll wait for you near the antenna, don't be afraid.

Put on the blindfold? Take off your coat, quick, light
the matches, put that corncob in your pocket.
Look, we'll eat it up here, we'll burn it. Don't be
afraid anymore, take off your coat. Look, I can fly!

With Broken Oars They Embarked

Statues, serenity of the sleigh
toward the mountains: how vulnerable
to certain love to be
lost on the landing without a banister!
Garden of the pit and the lightning bolt
where the diver suspended in air
is feverish...
and you, chalk-colored,
don't remove the winter
that descends in his voice: he is alive
like a nocturnal parchment, he breathes like a son.
Sky and earth
are calm, kneeling.

The Legend of Monferrato

The kingfishers
won in the lottery
have been frozen since January
but are still red
and there were
three madmen
who hid their hands
three brother bricklayers, thin
as poplar saplings,
three brothers
in the storm
and they spied an animal
with an earthly face, a snake
with the thinnest of bodies:
"I become huge, forever I become
s e r p e n t
kill me, you at least, kill me."

IV

A DISTANT FATHER

Year

Digging
toward a Lenten extreme
I was pushed
by the seed. Noon
overturned in its order.
Instinctively pure, every time, was
the hand stopped logically
between the snares
of that age and my mother's pain
I wasn't there, I didn't choose. The intercom issues
mental color
where the man is naked.
That drop
seen in three shares
became the only terrified substance, a
centuries-old ardor...
every pine tree...every pine...stop,
you are amid yourself.
Wheels withdrawing slowly
from the ice, a door's humility.

Line

To the head bobbing in the gunsight
we preferred an
illness of cold degrees and withdrawals: this too is
hate, I know, but this
twig turns idea pursued for
a year in limbo. And we, applause
faded, inhabited the night,
the elusive, marvelous springboard. Penetration
of sun in grain, which is mother. Survivor
whose name is father.

Telegram

The window remained as before. The cold
repeats that idiotic essence of rock
just as the letters of every word tremble.
Half smiling you point
out an exit, some stairs.
Not even now have you symbols for the dead.
I spoke to you of the sea, but the sea is a few square meters,
a drill, scarcely out. It was also, for us,
the intuition of a daughter breathing
in the first moments of a thing. Paper to say
broth and rice, months to say pillow. The blue ones call me
frozen in a fixed star.

Protect Me, My Talisman

Marta we found the cassette
that one morning she buried in the sand,
in the garden, in the keyboard, marta
an unfinished human figure carries
what remains of her accent, but
she always asked facing a window pane, but
we weren't there and the dress fell
to the asphalt marta there was a mark from
scarlet fever where the chest begins, the
double justice, the double cage,
the feathered mother we leave.

"On the Way to Mind"

Before the plums fell asleep
and the true paper turned blind
she withdrew feeling herself
struck and didn't recognize
the dog in the water...
it was her father...
he ran away from the kitchen
nodded
where the sky arrived
ripping the carbon paper
washing the glasses with ash
ducks like patriarchs
see that everything is in order
she pulled out her bathing suit
and showed it to the night
scales chase scales
the bandage has a strong odor of
fish soup
and the apron is locked inside her head:
she waited on the plane tree for

a long thought to end
then looked out the window
and while the grass was waiting
nine days passed in
June.

The Narrator

Judge of an abnormal stone,
in the heat of the piers, in the cold
of the elms. Slowly
the wrist turns
between the laser and sweet names for apricot
I too inhabit this revolving door
scouring the classified columns
with paintings for rent, cats given away,
I knock this obtuse cult,
teaching the alphabet with the same imagination
that obscures the other side to me.

Continuous Time

We were consigned
little boxes, identical,
filled with milk, from no maternity.
They are warnings and completeness,
they are scraps. In the hour of a notebook, this
dessicated notebook. "The eyes
don't find me." Warnings and completeness. Of the one
who accompanied us on terrafirma
we all preserve the style.

Hilbert's Program

I

We fell upon the chair
through a mistaken movement of the pen
clinging to grace,
our tobacco-stained grace.
We fell upon the balcony
where they threw salt. Ultraearthly,
a substance joined to the egg
scrutinizes the last days of oxygen.

II

On the right our
signature turning against us. On the left
a sirvente in dry-point:
"your daughter, alive, will assume the soul
of mine, who is dying."

The dancers call to us
in the body below, they possess
a silence and a turning
pencil of grass in the tall pencil.

III

Interior shelves, full of objects, collapse
in the bank. I see that scene again:
the dumbstruck people, the fast ones,
the corners and the scorching wire, strange rondo
of a word
at the climax of light and throat
"every pine tree...every pine...stop, you are amid
yourself . . ."

IV

Thus we made ours the remorse
of every thief; suspected,
we lived on incense
behind the crystal in the gynaeceum
we stare at the absolute middle
of a thing, a nutriment

repeated for decades, enclosed in the marrow
gathering on the ground fortune-telling
leaflets, little boxes for cats
which even when open set a limit for us.

V

The elevator cables sway, every thing
is divided into memory and mandrake.
First the dance with the snow. Then the processions
in repose like a masterpiece
whence to venture out barefoot. "In the water
whoever is silent isn't forgiven."
In the hour of a notebook, I answered:
if they were called there,
it was for some serious hell, a literary game
suicides sometimes play.
How many canteens given away as presents
before drowning, how much earth
spread upon the pillow!

VI

I squeezed the idea hard: and then marriage.
I rushed up to the fifth floor: and then I heard.
You were saying: goodbye passions
of hallucinated life, I want to light
a lamp, wake up here, feel
soft steps over my hands.
The day is that woman who
nurses against the wall, that zen
leaning. You were saying:
I looked at the part in my hair, I
turned back to the oil lamp, for the sages.

We children, we pine needles.

VII

"The water doesn't come back here, you find it again
in a throat."
At every turn of the earth,
the same face. No fissure
is as deep as those wrinkles. "Yes, you can
exchange my life for yours, if you want."

Head-sail, I called you. On an old slipway
you still sleep, stagger a little,
draw nine and a half meters with a free body.
Harsh begging
is the sign of twins...the migrating daughter,
the taciturn one from the hills: then the pollen
entered the dead and a supper appeared
in the dark, with friends.
She was there again,
in December, and it was the same one,
we could recognize her.

Finite Intuition

A nerve pivots and that space
seeks a scratch in the glue,
point outside page

"Where's
the earth you send spinning?"

I shall carry you on my shoulders,
complete cremation surrounded by posts:
suicides are more secretive than angels
and from the darkless side
the stitched nape will begin
the beginning

I shall carry you on my shoulders, in tatters, to
read, beyond the wall, beyond those

"The body was frost-bitten,
purple, devoid of essence."

Rowing in Familiar January

I heard from a friend: married. She was older
had a little hotel in Macerata,
he was open in the whitest fissure. In the letter
he spoke of filters to measure the blood
in winter. I remember the dirty cellophane,
the hand behind the glass. An alphabet creaks
hidden among the smooth overturned keels and
the photo-I.D. *There is a love greater*
than you and me, me and you in the species,
water over water.

Yearbook

From the barbed body, wires
climb into the air
with the proof of a scream. Like a
primitive formula of poverty,
every meal melts
into drops through the heart, every sleep
is encrusted in matter, that meeting
between raptus and firmament
wherefrom we return erased.

V

PROSE

Poetry and Theory

The Greek *theoria* signifies "reflection," but also "solemn embassy," "spectacle." And perhaps there can be no great poet who has not had theoretical insights into other great poets, who does not represent them on the stage of a conceptual power. Yet there is that pathetic mythology of the poet who—devoid of this power—nevertheless knows how to "tell a story" or to "dream," as if dream were the land where the thorn of intellect grows dull. It happens that some lines open the veins of their own thought until it is beyond recognition. But this clenched thought *must have been there*: only then can the lines enter the region which it doesn't know! This is delirium, in the most distinct accent of the calendar. Yet if those lines remain in doubt, if they are worried about not having thought enough...how much unworthy poetry of ideas is born from this worry...how many genuflections to philosophers... how many lines get cornered in the poetry of sensations. There should be no submission of theory to poetry, if they are Greek sisters. And no comparison, because these two strangers *must* have loved each other.

Starting a New Line:
An Autobiographical Note

Having immersed myself only recently (1977–1980) in the
iron arguments for starting a new line in poetry, I shall
attempt a quick history of this immersion. Perhaps my
first memory—from elementary school—is that familiar
one of the "laughing, fugitive" eyes of Silvia in Leopardi,
a subject on which a critic of the time held forth at great
length. He maintained how senseless it was to reverse the
two adjectives ("fugitive, laughing") because of the pre-
sumed risk of losing the feminine transience of a glance
which "demands that you slip into that fugitive ending."
Like my classmates, I immediately sensed the banality of
such an explanation, and with them I began to imagine
the beauty, the different beauty, of "fugitive, laughing."

Years later, while reading the hermetic poets, I noticed
the subtle attention paid to breaks and juxtapositions in
many verses of Mario Luzi (above all from *The Honor of
Truth*) or in the best Alfonso Gatto or in Piero Bigongiari.
(More than in others, where often the interruption seemed
contrived, accompanied by a solemnity that leaves open
mouths and hews to the rhetorical tradition most closely
bound to persuasion.) In fact, I recall two lines from
Bigongiari underlined in an old anthology—"Death is this/
glance fixed on your courtyards"—two lines in which the

caesura seemed and still seems to me inevitable: death is "this" and at the same time—after a silent interval—the "glance fixed on your courtyards," with that strange link between glance and fixity, two terms that don't agree, apparently, but which are wed in the totality of the poem. Later, after years in secondary school and university, I sought something else: a starting over even farther removed from meaning—from the meaning inherent in two separated lines and from that orchestral meaning which illuminates their separation—I sought, in other words, a rupture of the sentence that might be constrained by, but not derivable from, the sentence itself or the totality of the sentences. A rupture that might derive from a kind of dictation, which commanded both that the sentence be broken without explanation and that this break be loved in a total vision of poetry, although not of that poem: "total" being understood here as the whole of what pre-exists—a poetics—and of what is impending, a groping that *will become a poetics*.* By the same token, the term "dictation" does not in the least exclude infinite corrections or variants, scrupulously employed in the faithful repetition of what has been dictated. The variant is thus not a disobedience—never this, experimentalism finds it difficult—but on the contrary a more intense hearkening to the command, an "unexceptionable hearing."

* A Siberian legend relates: In a small village in the Byrranga mountains lived a woman who was the ugliest woman in the village. For years she remained shut inside her house, trying to appear in public as little as possible. But everyone was aware of her ugliness and could not stop them-

selves from avoiding her or simply, as with the most wicked
villagers, from deriding her pitilessly. The woman suffered
a great deal and one day decided to visit the wizard of the
village to see if he might do something for her. He asked
her to give him a few days, saying that a mysterious con-
coction of herbs could perform the miracle. When the
woman returned to the wizard, he announced, full of joy,
that the concoction was ready, and if she drank it, she
would appear the most beautiful of all the men and women
in the village, no one excluded, not even the malicious
ones. The woman agreed. She drank the potion, a mix-
ture of herbs she had never before tasted, and as she was
leaving the wizard's house, she realized the prophecy had
been fulfilled: everyone looked at her as if she were a
queen. For several days the happy woman walked proudly
through the entire village, much to the admiration of any-
one who met her. But gradually, as the weeks passed, a
worm began to gnaw at her mind. She thought: "Yes, it's
true, everyone finds me beautiful, *but in reality I am not*:
how shall I endure this secret my entire life?" With the
passage of time, the gnawing grew more and more bitter,
and the woman decided to return to the wizard to tell him
how much she suffered this discrepancy between the oth-
ers' gaze and her inner certainty that she was not beauti-
ful. But the wizard, like all the inhabitants of the village,
found her marvelous and could only express his admira-
tion to her over and over again: "you are beautiful, you
are the most beautiful one of all."

At this point, the legend ends, unresolved. The woman
thus finds herself suddenly alone and in an instant can
decide her life: whether to allow herself to be invented by
the others' gaze, to yield to this gaze, to accept the beauty
that is presented to her until she merges with it and is

beautiful by choice; or to preserve her sorrow, her terrible distinction between the others' gaze and her own. The woman chooses. This is what starting over means, among other things. A story unfolding inexorably, on the one hand. And on the other, a sudden rift, chained to that story and at the same time unaware that it is unfolding there.

The Absentees

Every manual of Italian literary history records a long void that runs more or less from the fifth century to the *Ritmo Laurenziano* and then to the thirteenth century: entire centuries were spent creating churches, paintings, and treatises and forgetting to leave us any poetry. The pages that describe these centuries are gray and lazy with the usual historico-economic interpretations, probing in various ways and with diverse subtlety the difficulties of a poetic birth. But then, several pages later, there is suddenly enthusiasm: St. Francis, Jacopone, Guittone, all the others appear. The absent now seem cast aside.

Thus it happens—prodigiously—that even a school manual can teach something, as soon as it refuses to beat its breast for those who could not, or represses any longing for a "history written by the victims," as the saying goes, leaving doubts as to whether the victims are the absent ones or those who collect alms so that no one will be absent.

Yet if someone shouts his love to you, how can you sew up his lips by listing all those who have not shouted it to you? Is there any greater cowardice? Think of Ariadne, when her thread leads Theseus to the mouth of the grotto. Theseus relates to her all his years in the labyrinth, the years when he could not embrace her. But outside, meanwhile, shines the Aegean, calling them unrelentingly.

Theseus temporizes, lingers over the joy he missed for so long, and winds up asking Ariadne to share in the darkness of his amputated years. And the Aegean continues to call, with its dense blue, so different from every other sea. It is here, then, that Ariadne, filled with love and disdain, cuts the thread and kills.

To the Swift Russian

The letters that Marina Tsvetayeva wrote to Pasternak
and Rilke in 1926 have a cutting and precise force, among
the most precise I have ever encountered in a correspon-
dence. They have a drive that knows no middle course,
not even in the face of her correspondents' most tempori-
zing responses. And at the same time they show an unex-
ceptionable sense of hearing, an offer to listen carried to
the point of philological spasm: a most pure intelligence
in its exclamations as well as at the microscope (and Rilke
grasps this literal listening, without ever mistaking
Tsvetayeva for an ordinary improviser). There are many
exclamations in Tsvetayeva's letters, and they all have a
clearly articulated necessity—and without any euphoric
confusion. If in Tsvetayeva the poet the exclamations at
times give in somewhat to their own effervescence, here
everything seems to marry her style and exclaim innately.
There is never a forewarning for effect or an invitation to
admire what is displayed: if any forewarnings appear, they
are humorous and laid bare with the childlike charm of
holding her breath. And there is a generous self-display,
capable of forgetting entirely certain hesitations from the
sick Rilke or certain simplistic commonplaces from
Pasternak; capable also, when confronting Rilke's verses,
of remaining firm and praising with equal force. Even
when Tsvetayeva sees that some things "are not possible"

(for instance, going to live with Pasternak in Moscow), her way of denying herself has something enthusiastic about it and does not yield at all to dejection: "Try to understand me: I am speaking of the ancient, insatiable hate of Psyche for Eve...I have another street, Boris, which flows along like a river, Boris, without people, with the endings of all ends, with a childhood, with everything but males."

But it is above all in the letters to Rilke that the drive is sharpened and offers inventions relentlessly. On the one hand, there is unqualified love for Rilke's poetry; on the other, a position far removed from that of a disciple: it is a love between blood relations who, united in poetry, no longer know reproach, even when they hate the unnecessary verse with an amputating fury: "Oh, Rainer, I don't want to choose (choosing is rooting, polluting!), I can not choose...Rainer! A book will follow *Craft*, there you will find a Saint George who is almost steed and a steed who is almost rider; I don't separate them and I name neither one. Your horseman! For a horseman is not the one who rides, horseman is the two together, a new figure, something that used not to be there, not knight and steed... Rainer, the purest happiness, a gift of happiness, pressing your forehead on the dog's forehead, eye to eye, and the dog, astonished, taken aback, and flattered (this doesn't happen every day!), growls. And then one holds his muzzle shut with both hands (since he might bite you from sheer emotion) and kisses, just smothers him." Then comes an increasingly urgent succession of words (this grows more extreme in August of 1926). What can Rilke say in response, if his awareness of his old age does not allow him to enter fully into this offering? Indeed, Rilke's replies have a lucid dignity and at times even a declared admiration ("from such pure self-sufficiency, out of the fullness and completeness of it all, you are right, and hence have forever a right to the infinite."). But he cannot bear a demand that leaves him so naked: in the end, even the noblest Rilkian dignity becomes a withdrawal (perhaps only Rimbaud's exclamation could not retreat before a demand so direct. But anyone who was loved by Tsvetayeva believed that in her challenge of words there must be, if only remotely, the pretense of sharing a story between private individuals.). And yet even in the face of Rilke's tormenting withdrawal, Tsvetayeva is not reproachful. Her ear for his poetry always remains sharp, ready to sing of its unforgiving beauty.

Finally, after the German poet's death, another letter: "No, you are not yet faraway and high above, you are right here, with your head on my shoulder. You will never be faraway: never inaccessibly high" (31 December 1926).

Psychotropic Substances

Anyone who, at any moment in his life, has found himself under the influence of some substance and grasped several unappreciated aspects of language can only smile at the mediocrity of the literature about drugs and be compelled to save very few things: Artaud's *To the Land of the Tarahumara*, some pages from Henri Michaux. And yet there is a fantastic algebra—when it is read outside of any bacchic frenzy—in pharmacology, in the study of drug interactions, in the impossibility of "adding up" their effects, in the relations of transference that form among the substances themselves. In this sense, it is more interesting to read the four prolix volumes of Aiazzi and Donatelli—their *Treatise on Pharmacology*—than all the work of Burroughs or Ginsberg, to say nothing of Timothy Leary. But it is equally clear that those four volumes are not enough, that they are only a primer for entering into the latticework of the neurology, and then reading the chemistry without any neurology. There are substances—phendimetrazine, methylphenidate (ritalin), prolintane, phencanphamine—very far removed from alcoholic familiarity, powerfully concentrated on the word and its uniqueness, far too from the unbalanced game of hallucinogens and other mind-altering drugs, and far, finally, from the distinctive tachycardiac gesturing of a true and proper amphetamine. Those substances leave no escape before a written line of poetry: one must stop there, even for hours, until it cannot but exist. The lesson they teach can also not require further experiments, quite like one's loyalty to a favorite flavor or food. To enter the game of substances— to enter it without a stereotypical idea of feeling well or ill—demands the same logical digging that a line of poetry can demand: with no gratitude and no reward. The structural formula that managed to penetrate the numbers of the body was already part of a myth. Now it is simply discovered: there was no trip, whether good or bad. Why justify it, then? Yet rarely have poets spoken of the substances they used, when this connection was relevant: the drug was decanted in the lines, necessary but no longer recognizable, silent handmaiden of poetry.

Twentieth-Century Tragedy

At times the calendar's page proves leaden, refusing to be turned, provoking a sudden decision. Then tragedy—which obviously has nothing to do with the doleful finale—becomes the moment of a decision without future or assistance. It is a "foreign" moment—as Paul Celan writes—in which the intellect plummets along the body and pierces the feet; but it is also the auroral moment in which, through this piercing, contact is made with agriculture. Here the blood that flows from the pierced feet of the crucified Christ to bathe the earth is related to Demeter, fertile goddess of the fields. The tragic creature is therefore a thesis (in the Hegelian sense) overcome by a synthesis. And if drama is the investigation of an antithesis, tragedy stands out more and more clearly as the vertical collapse of this investigation: it is the very moment in which one can't temporize, can't save the saveable, not even by resorting to the expedient of suicide, or another arbitrary gesture. Hegel insists that there is no tragedy in the purely arbitrary act, without the barrier of some limit: "Tragedy is that collision between the arbitrary and its stockade."

The few tragic poets of twentieth-century Europe reveal precisely the identity between tragedy and contempt for a remedy. In effect, confronted with the sense of an error that is impending but still obscure, one can clear a path: the remedy of exempting oneself. But in the very moment that this path is entered, difficulty takes its revenge, and the path itself increasingly looms as error or sin: a venial sin which, intertwined with absolution, definitively precludes that leaden page. If, therefore, tragedy is the decision to avoid indulgence, its relationship with Orphism past and present becomes increasingly tenuous. To maintain the contrary has implied the cancellation of the purgatorial element that continually emerges in Orphism, particularly in the belief in an after-life of reward and punishment meted out according to the degree of the soul's purity during its earthly life. (This does not exclude the fact that Purgatory, with a pull on the purifying thread, can afford a glimpse of harshness—that of Dante's Beatrice in Canto XXXI—and least of all does it exclude the tragic consistency of several Old Testament prophets overcome by God to the point of hating him.)

But every variant of Stoicism certainly appears incompatible with tragedy, from the Senecan caricature of *fata nolentem trahunt, volentem ducunt* (in tragedy, in fact, what customarily happens is that *volentem trahunt*!) to the existentialist philosophies most crammed with Stoic gestures which, reducing tragedy to the evil of living, withstand the blows of existence with the badge of the stigmata (or, more banally, bruises). This is the easiest way to mitigate the collision between telos and contingency. It is a solution strongly refuted by tragedians from Aeschylus to Celan, if tragedy is what continues to end.

Notes

The Italian texts from which this translation was made were chosen to provide a representative selection of De Angelis's writing. The poems have been drawn from his four collections and grouped into sections that correspond to the order in which the books were published: *Somiglianze* (*Resemblances*, 1976), *Millimetri* (*Millimeters*, 1983), *Terra del viso* (*Land of the Face*, 1985), and *Distante un padre* (*A Distant Father*, 1989). The prose pieces which constitute the fifth section have been drawn from De Angelis's collection of critical and theoretical essays, *Poesia e destino* (*Poetry and Fate*, 1982). Much of the information provided in the following notes relies on conversations and correspondence with the poet.

GEE
The title of the Italian text, "Stineda," is a nonsense word used here to signify a child's shout of amazement.

THE SLOWNESS
This poem records an incident that occurred on the out-
skirts of Brno in Czechoslovakia. "Jezkova" is a street in
Prague. The word *nerozumím* is Czech for "I don't under-
stand."

NOON GLARE
The title of the Italian text is "La luce sulle tempie," in
English "The Light on the Temples [i.e., the sides of the
head]."

'A.S.'
The title of the Italian text is "'T.S.'," a medical abbrevia-
tion used to designate patients who have attempted sui-
cide ("tentato suicidio").

THE CANES
The image of the canes smashing the bucket alludes to a
rural marriage ritual, a ritual of divination, which takes
various forms in the different regions of Italy. In the Pied-
mont, the most beautiful girl in the village, when she has
reached eighteen, is blindfolded and led in front of two
buckets, one empty, the other filled with coins. If with the
first blow of the cane she strikes the bucket with the coins,
they become her dowry, and the first man to catch one of
them can ask for her hand. If she rejects him, she loses the
money, but is given one coin to throw to the man she
wishes.

LETTER FROM VIGNOLE
Vignole is a town near the Austrian border where Marta
Bertamini, De Angelis's friend and collaborator, was born.

IN HISTORY

The first two lines of the Italian text translate the opening of Paul Celan's poem "Radix, Matrix" from *Die Niemandsrose* (1963): "As one speaks to stone, like/you" ("Wie man zum Stein spricht, wie/du").

RONEFOR

The title is the name of a basketball arena in Sesto San Giovanni, a suburb of Milan that is the site of foundries, mills, glassworks, and chemical factories. The word also resembles the name of an Indian boy with whom De Angelis often travelled to this suburb.

VIA PROSPERO FINZI

The title is a street in Milan which contains some deserted buildings and is now a haunt of prostitutes.

CONVERSATION WITH FATHER

This poem refers to stories about the Italian Resistance during World War II which De Angelis was told in his childhood by his father.

FOREWEB

The title of the Italian text, "Antela," is a neologism which combines "antenati" ("forebears") and "ragnatela" ("spider web").

THE LEGEND OF MONFERRATO

Monferrato is a rural area in the Piedmont where De Angelis lived as a child.

'ON THE WAY TO MIND'

Verso la mente (*On the Way to Mind*) is the title of a col-

lection of poems by De Angelis's friend, Nadia Campana,
posthumously published in 1990.

HILBERT'S PROGRAM
David Hilbert (1862–1943) was a German mathematician
who sought a theoretical foundation for mathematics
which would solve what he viewed as key research prob-
lems without leading to contradiction.

STARTING A NEW LINE:
AN AUTOBIOGRAPHICAL NOTE
Mario Luzi (b. 1914), Alfonso Gatto (1909–1976), and Piero
Bigongiari (b. 1913) are poets and critics associated with
the "hermetic" movement in modern Italian poetry. Cen-
tered in Florence during the 1930s and 1940s, the hermetic
poets reacted against the traditional forms and rhetoric
cultivated by turn-of-the-century Italian writers like
Giosue Carducci, Giovanni Pascoli, and Gabriel D'Annunzio;
they took different models—the French symbolists, the
fragmented terseness of Giuseppe Ungaretti's early po-
ems (1919), the abrupt shifts between image and comment
in Eugenio Montale's first two collections (1925 and 1939).
Hermeticism is characterized by precise, elliptical lan-
guage, dense images, free verse, formal elements that con-
stitute a typically modern poetics of indirection, giving
these texts their often noted "hermetic" or obscure qual-
ity. Luzi's collection *The Honor of Truth* appeared in 1957.
De Angelis quotes from Bigongiari's poem "Pescia-Lucca,"
included in his 1958 collection *The Walls of Pistoia*.

THE ABSENTEES
The *Ritmo Laurenziano* ("Laurentian Verse," named af-
ter the Biblioteca Laurenziano in Florence where it was

discovered) is the oldest surviving poetic composition in the Italian vernacular. Written between 1150 and 1170, it is the work of a troubadour who requests the gift of a horse from a bishop. "St. Francis, Jacopone, Guittone" are the first figures in the canon of medieval Italian literature; they indicate cultural trends in Northern Italy during this period. The poetry of St. Francis of Assisi (1182–1226), founder of the Order of Franciscan Brothers, is noted for the lyrical simplicity of its nature mysticism. Jacopone da Todi (c. 1230/36–1306), who joined the Franciscans as a lay brother, wrote devotional poetry which reflects his extreme asceticism and his episodes of ecstatic madness. Guittone d'Arezzo (1235–1294), a participant in the violent political struggles of thirteenth-century Tuscany, later joined the Brothers of the Virgin Mary; he wrote highly rhetorical poems on moral, religious and political themes.

TO THE SWIFT RUSSIANS
The quotations from Tsvetayeva and Rilke follow the English versions in Boris Pasternak, Marina Tsvetayeva, and Rainer Maria Rilke, *Letters: Summer 1926*, ed. Yevgeny Pasternak, Yelena Pasternak, and Konstantin M. Azadovsky, trans. Margaret Wettlin and Walter Arndt (San Diego: Harcourt Brace Jovanovich, 1985).

TWENTIETH-CENTURY TRAGEDY
In the reference to the "'foreign' moment," De Angelis quotes from the closing lines of Celan's poem "Schliere" ("Streak") in *Sprachgitter* (1959):

> Streak in the eye:
> that a sign, borne through
> the dark, be proved there,
> from the sand (or ice?) of a foreign

time for a more foreign Always
lived and as a mute
quivering consonant voiced.

("Schliere im Aug:/ dass bewahrt sei/ ein durchs Dunkel
getragenes Zeichen,/ vom Sand (oder Eis?) einer fremden/
Zeit fur ein fremderes Immer/ belebt und als stumm/
vibrierender Mitlaut gestimmt.")

The Latin sentence reads, "Fate drags the unwilling, leads
the willing."

Milo De Angelis

Milo De Angelis was born in Milan on 6 June 1951. He spent his childhood in Monferrato, a village in the Piedmont. The childhood experiences of this rural setting, the agrarian practices, the proximity of nature, the provincial legends, would later prove formative to his poetry, reinforcing a central thematic preoccupation with the natural cycle as well as contributing a number of autobiographical allusions. During his late teens, De Angelis became deeply involved in sport, initially soccer, later track and field. These experiences would also reemerge in his poetry as a pattern of athletic images that resonate with his philosophical speculations. He studied at the University of Milan from 1970 to 1974 and then at the University of Montpellier from 1975 to 1976, receiving a degree in contemporary Italian literature and classical philology.

De Angelis began writing poetry at an early age, in his mid-teens, when he was also beginning his wide readings in literature, philosophy, and literary criticism. His precocious debut occurred in 1975, when some of his poems appeared in two anthologies important in the history of contemporary Italian poetry: the prestigious annual *L'almanacco dello Specchio* (*The Almanack of the Mirror*), which usually prints a few interesting newcomers along with recent work by respected major writers; and *Il pubblico della poesia* (*The Audience of Poetry*), a selection of twenty-five poets designed to characterize the social and cultural situation of Italian poetry in the 1970s. In 1976, De Angelis published his first collection of poems, *Somiglianze* (*Resemblances*) with the small press Guanda, noted for its list of experimental writing. These first publications signalled his emergence as a key figure in post-World War II Italian poetry, one who was developing in new ways the experimentalism initiated by such groups as the *Novissimi* and *Gruppo 63* in the 1950s and 1960s. De Angelis's poetry shows a commitment to the formal innovation championed by this experimentalist movement, but in the service of speculation on the nature of language and human subjectivity influenced by Nietzsche and Heidegger, Bataille and Blanchot, Lacan and Deleuze. The result, in the words of the poet and critic Maurizio Cucchi, is that "idea and freedom of image often coexist in his verses, revealing a subtending, insinuating uneasiness, an always arduous and troubling skewing of experience."

In the late 1970s, De Angelis's researches in poetry and philosophy led to his founding of the journal *niebo* (1976–80) and to his translation of several pertinent texts, Blanchot's *L'attente l'oubli*, Baudelaire's *Paradis artificiels*, and, with Marta Bertamini, Claudianus' *De raptu de Proserpine*. In 1982, De Angelis offered a provocative glimpse of his thinking in *Poesia e destino* (*Poetry and Fate*), a collection of critical and theoretical essays in which he addressed a wide range of texts, European and Eastern, classical and modern. Throughout the 1980s, he lived in Milan, tutoring private students in Greek and Latin literature while writing the poems that brilliantly confirmed his early promise, attracting the attention of Italy's most respected publishers and critics. His second collection, *Millimetri* (*Millimeters*) appeared in

1983 from Einaudi, his third, *Terra del viso* (*Land of the Face*), in 1985 and his fourth, *Distante un padre* (*A Distant Father*), in 1989, both from Mondadori. In 1990, Guanda released a new, revised edition of *Somiglianze*, recognizing its status as a contemporary classic. De Angelis is married to the poet Giovanna Sicari, and they have a son, Daniele. Currently they live in Rome.

*

Lawrence Venuti was born in Philadelphia in 1953. He received a Ph.D. from Columbia University in 1980 and is currently professor of English at Temple University. He is the author of *Our Halcyon Dayes: English Prerevolutionary Texts and Postmodern Culture* (Wisconsin, 1989) and *The Translator's Invisibility* (Routledge, 1995). He is also the editor of *Rethinking Translation: Discourse, Subjectivity, Ideology* (Routledge, 1992). His translations from the Italian include Barbara Alberti's novel *Delirium* (Farrar, Straus & Giroux, 1980), the architect Aldo Rossi's *Scientific Autobiography* (MIT, 1981), *Restless Nights: Selected Stories of Dino Buzzati* (North Point, 1983), and I. U. Tarchetti's *Fantastic Tales* (Mercury House, 1992) and *Passion* (Mercury House, 1994). His translations and reviews of Italian writing have appeared in such periodicals as *Conjunctions*, *Harper's*, *The New York Times Book Review*, *The Philadelphia Inquirer*, *Poetry*, and *Sulfur*. He has won the PEN American Center's Renato Poggioli Award for Italian Translation and held grants from the National Endowment for the Arts and the National Endowment for the Humanities. He is the General Editor of Border Lines: Works in Translation, a book series from Temple University Press.

SUN & MOON CLASSICS

This publication was made possible, in part, through an operational grant from the Andrew W. Mellon Foundation and through contributions from the following individuals:

Charles Altieri (Seattle, Washington)
John Arden (Galway, Ireland)
Paul Auster (Brooklyn, New York)
Jesse Huntley Ausubel (New York, New York)
Dennis Barone (West Hartford, Connecticut)
Jonathan Baumbach (Brooklyn, New York)
Guy Bennett (Los Angeles, California)
Bill Berkson (Bolinas, California)
Steve Benson (Berkeley, California)
Charles Bernstein and Susan Bee (New York, New York)
Dorothy Bilik (Silver Spring, Maryland)
Alain Bosquet (Paris, France)
In Memoriam: John Cage
In Memoriam: Camilo José Cela
Bill Corbett (Boston, Massachusetts)
Fielding Dawson (New York, New York)
Robert Crosson (Los Angeles, California)
Tina Darragh and P. Inman (Greenbelt, Maryland)
Christopher Dewdney (Toronto, Canada)
Arkadii Dragomoschenko (St. Petersburg, Russia)
George Economou (Norman, Oklahoma)
Kenward Elmslie (Calais, Vermont)
Elaine Equi and Jerome Sala (New York, New York)
Lawrence Ferlinghetti (San Francisco, California)
Richard Foreman (New York, New York)
Howard N. Fox (Los Angeles, California)
Jerry Fox (Aventura, Florida)
In Memoriam: Rose Fox
Melvyn Freilicher (San Diego, California)
Miro Gavran (Zagreb, Croatia)
Allen Ginsberg (New York, New York)
Peter Glassgold (Brooklyn, New York)
Barbara Guest (New York, New York)
Perla and Amiram V. Karney (Bel Air, California)

Fred Haines (Los Angeles, California)
Václav Havel (Prague, The Czech Republic)
Lyn Hejinian (Berkeley, California)
Fanny Howe (La Jolla, California)
Harold Jaffe (San Diego, California)
Ira S. Jaffe (Albuquerque, New Mexico)
Pierre Joris (Albany, New York)
Alex Katz (New York, New York)
Tom LaFarge (New York, New York)
Mary Jane Lafferty (Los Angeles, California)
Michael Lally (Santa Monica, California)
Norman Lavers (Jonesboro, Arkansas)
Jerome Lawrence (Malibu, California)
Stacey Levine (Seattle, Washington)
Herbert Lust (Greenwich, Connecticut)
Norman MacAffee (New York, New York)
Rosemary Macchiavelli (Washington, DC)
Beatrice Manley (Los Angeles, California)
In Memoriam: Mary McCarthy
Harry Mulisch (Amsterdam, The Netherlands)
Iris Murdoch (Oxford, England)
Martin Nakell (Los Angeles, California)
In Memoriam: bpNichol
Toby Olson (Philadelphia, Pennsylvania)
Maggie O'Sullivan (Hebden Bridge, England)
Rochelle Owens (Norman, Oklahoma)
Marjorie and Joseph Perloff (Pacific Palisades, California)
Dennis Phillips (Los Angeles, California)
Carl Rakosi (San Francisco, California)
Tom Raworth (Cambridge, England)
David Reed (New York, New York)
Ishmael Reed (Oakland, California)
Janet Rodney (Santa Fe, New Mexico)
Joe Ross (Washington, DC)
Jerome and Diane Rothenberg (Encinitas, California)
Dr. Marvin and Ruth Sackner (Miami Beach, Florida)
Floyd Salas (Berkeley, California)
Tom Savage (New York, New York)
Leslie Scalapino (Oakland, California)
James Sherry (New York, New York)
Aaron Shurin (San Francisco, California)

Charles Simic (Strafford, New Hampshire)
Gilbert Sorrentino (Stanford, California)
Catharine R. Stimpson (Staten Island, New York)
John Taggart (Newburg, Pennsylvania)
Nathaniel Tarn (Tesuque, New Mexico)
Fiona Templeton (New York, New York)
Mitch Tuchman (Los Angeles, California)
Hannah Walker and Ceacil Eisner (Orlando, Florida)
Wendy Walker (New York, New York)
Anne Walter (Carnac, France)
Jeffery Weinstein (New York, New York)
Mac Wellman (Brooklyn, New York)
Arnold Wesker (Hay on Wye, England)

If you would like to be a contributor to this series, please send your tax-deductible contribution to The Contemporary Arts Educational Project, Inc., a non-profit corporation, 6026 Wilshire Boulevard, Los Angeles, California 90036.

SUN & MOON CLASSICS

Author	Title
Alferi, Pierre	*Natural Gait* 95 ($10.95)
Antin, David	*Selected Poems: 1963–1973* 10 ($12.95)
Barnes, Djuna	*At the Roots of the Stars: The Short Plays* 53 ($12.95)
	The Book of Repulsive Women 59 ($6.95)
	Interviews 86 ($13.95)
	New York 5 ($12.95)
	Smoke and Other Early Stories 2 ($10.95)
Bernstein, Charles	*Content's Dream: Essays 1975–1984* 49 ($14.95)
	Dark City 48 ($11.95)
	Rough Trades 14 ($10.95)
Bjørneboe, Jens	*The Bird Lovers* 43 ($9.95)
Breton, André	*Arcanum 17* 51 ($12.95)
	Earthlight 26 ($12.95)
Bromige, David	*The Harbormaster of Hong Kong* 32 ($10.95)
Butts, Mary	*Scenes from the Life of Cleopatra* 72 ($13.95)
Cadiot, Olivier	*L'Art Poétique* 98 ($10.95)
Celan, Paul	*Breathturn* 74 ($12.95)
Coolidge, Clark	*The Crystal Text* 99 ($11.95)
	Own Face 39 ($10.95)
	The Rova Improvisations 34 ($11.95)
Copioli, Rosita	*The Blazing Lights of the Sun* 84 ($11.95)
De Angelis, Milo	*Finite Intuition* 65 ($11.95)
DiPalma, Ray	*Numbers and Tempers: Selected Early Poems* 24 (11.95)
von Doderer, Heimito	*The Demons* 13 ($29.95)
	Every Man a Murderer 66 ($14.95)

Jenkin, Len   *Careless Love*   54   ($9.95)

Dark Ride and Other Plays   22   ($13.95)

Jensen, Wilhelm   *Gradiva*   38   ($13.95)

Jones, Jeffrey M.   *Love Trouble*   78   ($9.95)

Katz, Steve   *43 Fictions*   18   ($12.95)

Larbaud, Valery   *Childish Things*   19   ($13.95)

Lins, Osman   *Nine, Novena*   104   ($13.95

Mac Low, Jackson   *Pieces O' Six*   17   ($11.95)

Marinetti, F. T.   *Let's Murder the Moonshine:*
       Selected Writings   12   ($12.95)

The Untameables   28   ($11.95)

Messerli, Douglas, ed.   *50: A Celebration of Sun & Moon Classics*
       50   ($13.95)

From the Other Side of the Century: A New
       American Poetry 1960–1990   47   ($29.95)

Morley, Christopher   *Thunder on the Left*   68   ($12.95)

Nerval, Gérard de   *Aurélia*   103   ($12.95)

Novarina, Valere   *The Theater of the Ears*   85   ($13.95)

North, Charles   *Shooting for Line: New and Selected Poems*
       102   ($12.95)

Pacheco, José Emilio   *A Distant Death*   41   ($21.95, cloth)

Porta, Antonio   *Metropolis*   73   ($10.95)

Propertius, Sextus   *Charm*   89   ($11.95)

Queneau, Raymond   *The Children of Limon*   92   ($13.95)

Rakosi, Carl   *Poems 1923–1941*   64   ($12.95)

Raworth, Tom   *Eternal Sections*   23   ($9.95)

Romero, Norberto Luis   *The Arrival of Autumn in Constantinople*
       105   ($12.95)

Roselli, Amelia   *War Variations*   81   ($11.95)

Rothenberg, Jerome   *Gematria*   45   ($11.95)

Sarduy, Severo   *From Cuba with a Song*   52   ($10.95)

Scalapino, Leslie   *Defoe*   46   ($11.95)

Schnitzler, Arthur   *Dream Story*   6   ($10.95)

Lieutenant Gustl   37   ($9.95)